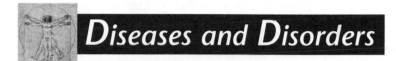

Diseases and Disorders

Multiple Sclerosis

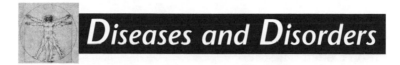

Diseases and Disorders

Multiple Sclerosis

Titles in the Diseases and Disorders series include:

Diseases and Disorders

Multiple Sclerosis

by Melissa Abramovitz

LUCENT
BOOKS®

THOMSON
GALE

San Diego • Detroit • New York • San Francisco • Cleveland
New Haven, Conn. • Waterville, Maine • London • Munich

LIBRARY OF CONGRESS CATALOGING-IN-PUBLICATION DATA

Abramovitz, Melissa, 1954—
    Multiple sclerosis / by Melissa Abramovitz.
        v. cm. — (Diseases and disorders)
Includes bibliographical references and index.
Contents: What is multiple sclerosis? — What causes multiple sclerosis? — How is multiple
sclerosis treated? — Living with multiple sclerosis — The Future.
    ISBN 1-59018-042-9
    1. Multiple sclerosis—Juvenile literature. [1. Multiple sclerosis. 2. Diseases.] I. Title.
II. Series.
    RC377 .A273 2003
    616.8' 34—dc21

                                                                        2002007893

Printed in the United States of America

Table of Contents

"The Most Difficult Puzzles Ever Devised"

CHARLES BEST, ONE of the pioneers in the search for a cure for diabetes, once explained what it is about medical research that intrigued him so. "It's not just the gratification of knowing one is helping people," he confided, "although that probably is a more heroic and selfless motivation. Those feelings may enter in, but truly, what I find best is the feeling of going toe to toe with nature, of trying to solve the most difficult puzzles ever devised. The answers are there somewhere, those keys that will solve the puzzle and make the patient well. But how will those keys be found?"

Since the dawn of civilization, nothing has so puzzled people—and often frightened them, as well—as the onset of illness in a body or mind that had seemed healthy before. A seizure, the inability of a heart to pump, the sudden deterioration of muscle tone in a small child—being unable to reverse such conditions or even to understand why they occur was unspeakably frustrating to healers. Even before there were names for such conditions, even before they were understood at all, each was a reminder of how complex the human body was, and how vulnerable.

While our grappling with understanding diseases has been frustrating at times, it has also provided some of humankind's most heroic accomplishments. Alexander Fleming's accidental discovery in 1928 of a mold that could be turned into penicillin has resulted in the saving of untold millions of lives. The isolation of the enzyme insulin has reversed what was once a death sentence for anyone with diabetes. There have been great strides in combating conditions for which there is not yet a cure, too. Medicines can help AIDS patients live longer, diagnostic tools such as mammography and ultrasounds can help doctors find tumors while they are treatable, and laser surgery techniques have made the most intricate, minute operations routine.

This "toe-to-toe" competition with diseases and disorders is even more remarkable when seen in a historical continuum. An astonishing amount of progress has been made in a very short time. Just two hundred years ago, the existence of germs as a cause of some diseases was unknown. In fact, it was less than 150 years ago that a British surgeon named Joseph Lister had difficulty persuading his fellow doctors that washing their hands before delivering a baby might increase the chances of a healthy delivery (especially if they had just attended to a diseased patient)!

Each book in Lucent's *Diseases and Disorders* series explores a disease or disorder and the knowledge that has been accumulated (or discarded) by doctors through the years. Each book also examines the tools used for pinpointing a diagnosis, as well as the various means that are used to treat or cure a disease. Finally, new ideas are presented—techniques or medicines that may be on the horizon.

Frustration and disappointment are still part of medicine, for not every disease or condition can be cured or prevented. But the limitations of knowledge are being pushed outward constantly; the "most difficult puzzles ever devised" are finding challengers every day.

An Unpredictable and Incurable Disease

Multiple sclerosis takes each person it strikes on a frightening journey into uncharted territory. Even though experts know what types of people get multiple sclerosis, also known as MS, most often no one can predict who will develop this debilitating disease of the central nervous system. For example, MS generally begins between the ages of fifteen and forty-five, but it can start at a much younger or older age. It strikes women two to three times as often as men, but many men get the disease too. Caucasians are affected more frequently than other racial groups, but MS occurs in all racial groups to some extent. Most people who get multiple sclerosis live in northern areas of the globe or in regions far south of the equator, but no one knows why this happens, and anyone in any geographic location can develop the disorder at any time.

Different Paths for Different People

Once a diagnosis of MS has been made, doctors are unable to predict how the disease will progress. Some patients experience fairly mild symptoms that do not impair their activities to a great extent. Others have unrelenting pain, paralysis, and varying degrees of disability that leave them confined to a bed or a wheelchair, dependent on others for help with simple tasks. In addition, the symptoms of MS may worsen without warning

A young boy with multiple sclerosis sits at his desk in a wheelchair.

from hour to hour or day to day; this makes it difficult to schedule activities and make long-term plans.

Multiple sclerosis experts do not yet understand why the disease varies so much in different individuals. According to the authors of *Multiple Sclerosis: A Guide for the Newly Diagnosed,*

> We do not know why one person has a progressive course of symptoms and problems, while another has mild disease that produces little disability throughout the lifespan. It can have different patterns in people in the same family and what patterns a person has seems to have nothing to do with anything we can measure in their bodies, their life activities, or whatever steps they take to change things.[1]

Patients and their families, as well as doctors, find the unpredictable nature of MS to be one of the most frustrating things about the disorder. Amy, a young woman who developed MS in her twenties, explains: "I think not knowing what will happen is the hardest thing for people when they're diagnosed with MS. They totally freak out and wonder 'What's the disease going to do to me?' They have to realize that what happens to someone else is not necessarily going to happen to them. And if it does, well, you will have to deal with it."[2]

An Incurable Disease of the Brain

The journey into this unpredictable disorder is made more frightening by the fact that the brain is the most important organ in the body. Even minor damage to it can affect how a person thinks, feels, moves, and otherwise lives. Although diseases that impact other essential organs like the heart or kidneys can have serious consequences, conditions that harm the brain are especially unsettling to human beings. "In many ways, diseases that affect our brains are more frightening than diseases affecting other parts of our bodies. A neurological (affecting the nervous system) disease may affect everything about me,"[3] says Dr. Roger S. Cicala in his book *The Brain Disorders Sourcebook.*

Add this fear of brain malfunctions to the reality that MS is incurable at this time, and the stressful experience is intensified into a lifelong challenge. People who live with the disease say knowing that it will not go away or be rendered inert by a pill or surgical operation totally alters one's outlook. Joe, an attorney who was diagnosed with MS in his twenties, states, "When I was a kid and was sick or injured, the doctor gave me medicine or stitched me up. Even when I took a knee in the back in a ball game and was out for a month, I healed. That's what illness was: Something you fixed." But these perceptions were badly disrupted when he developed MS: "It was unimaginable to me that I had something incurable. Incurable wasn't part of my vocabulary."[4]

Hope for the Journey Ahead

Despite being faced with an incurable and unpredictable disorder, MS patients today have reason for hope. For the first time in history, doctors are able to slow the disease process in some people and treat many symptoms with drugs to allow patients to lead fairly long and fulfilling lives. Hundreds of researchers through-

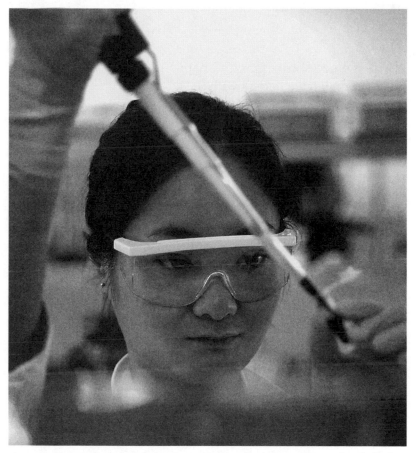

A researcher prepares a dose of an experimental drug designed to halt the progress of multiple sclerosis.

out the world are currently making huge strides toward understanding the underlying causes of MS and in developing new, more effective treatment methods; indeed, the possibility of curing the disease looks more realistic all the time. Says Labe C. Scheinberg, professor emeritus of neurology at Albert Einstein College of Medicine in New York, "Never before has there been so positive an outlook for the future as the result of research that has led to the development of new treatments designed to prevent progression of the disease and that hold out the hope of that most elusive target, a cure for what was previously regarded as incurable."[5]

Chapter 1

What Is Multiple Sclerosis?

Multiple sclerosis is a chronic disease of the central nervous system—the brain and spinal cord. It currently affects about 2 million people worldwide and about 300,000 in the United States.

Some controversy exists over whether the disease has been around throughout human history or just within the past two hundred or so years. Although ancient historical documents contain descriptions of illnesses with symptoms similar to those seen in MS, doctors are not certain whether the patients described were actually afflicted with multiple sclerosis or with another disorder that shares some of its characteristics.

Whether multiple sclerosis has existed for thousands of years or just in recent centuries, it was not formally described as a disease until 1835. Medical historians attribute the first recognized clinical description to an 1835 textbook by Dr. Jean Cruveilhier, a professor at the Faculty of Medicine in Paris, France. Cruveilhier discussed several patients with progressively weak, unresponsive limbs, vision problems, muscle spasms, and assorted other symptoms and noted that examination of the patients' spinal cords revealed gray areas of scar tissue that he called *taches*, which is French for "spots." He referred to the disorder as *"paraplégie par degeneration grise des cordons de la moelle,"*[6] meaning "paralysis by degeneration of the gray fibers of the spinal cord."

The Disease Gets an Official Name

Few doctors outside France had access to Cruveilhier's writings, however, and thus few recognized the collection of symptoms now associated with MS as a single disease entity. The disorder itself did not even receive a formal name until 1868, when Dr. Jean Martin Charcot of the Salpétrière Hospital in Paris gave it the official name of *sclérose en plaques,* which means "patches of scars," based on the results of autopsies he conducted on patients who had succumbed to the disease. This name is still used in French-speaking countries.

Charcot, who is known as the father of neurology (the branch of medicine relating to the nervous system), also made detailed descriptions of the nervous system damage that accompanied *sclérose en plaques.* His lectures and drawings on the subject brought the disease to the attention of doctors throughout the world and led to its classification as a specific neurological disorder, like epilepsy or cerebral palsy.

After extensive research, Dr. Jean Martin Charcot was the first to formally indentify MS in 1868.

American neurologist William Alexander Hammond is credited with giving the disease multiple sclerosis its English name.

Once doctors worldwide became familiar with the disease, it was officially named in other languages besides French. *Sclérose en plaques* was first referred to as disseminated, or insular, sclerosis in America by Dr. Edward Seguin during the mid-1870s. The first word emphasizes the fact that the characteristic areas of scarring in the nervous system are distributed (disseminated) in places throughout the brain and spinal cord. The word *insular* highlights the isletlike appearance of the various patches of scar tissue. And the American physician followed his French colleague by using *sclerosis* (from the Greek word *skleros*, which means "hard") to describe the hardened scar tissue found in patients with the disease.

Medical historians credit the American neurologist William A. Hammond with the first known use of the term *multiple cerebral sclerosis*, which was later shortened to *multiple sclerosis* and remains the official name in English-speaking countries. It literally means "many hardened scars."

Scars in the Nervous System

Modern physicians have a much better understanding of the scar tissue involved in MS than did doctors during the 1800s, though

Charcot's original drawings and descriptions are still considered accurate and remained state-of-the-art knowledge in medical textbooks for many decades.

Once doctors had the sophisticated technology necessary for viewing the tiny cells that compose this scar tissue, they were able to ascertain that it is primarily made up of T lymphocytes, B lymphocytes, plasma cells, and oligodendrocytes. T and B lymphocytes and plasma cells are kinds of white blood cells. Like all white blood cells, they are important in the body's immune system. Oligodendrocytes nourish and support the nerve cells, or neurons, that run the brain and the entire body.

Neurons are composed of a cell body containing parts that keep the cell alive, a long branch called an axon, and one or more thinner branches known as dendrites. Groups of nerve cell bodies clustered together in the brain have a grayish color and are known as the gray matter of the brain. Groups or bundles of axons and dendrites are covered by a white protective fatty shield and are thus known as the white matter of the brain.

Oligodendrocytes manufacture and wrap this all-important white fatty shield around the axons and dendrites that it protects. The shield is called the myelin sheath. Damage to this sheath results in the characteristic symptoms of multiple sclerosis. Repeated inflammation of myelin leads to its destruction, a process called demyelination. For this reason, MS is classified as a demyelinating disease.

Wherever it occurs, demyelination leaves areas of scarring, known as plaques or lesions. They tend to be gray in color, as Cruveilhier and Charcot noted in their original descriptions of MS.

Garbled Messages

The myelin sheath normally acts like the insulation around an electrical wire. Its job is to protect the neurons' electrical impulses as they travel throughout the body. Normally, these nerve impulses travel at about 225 miles per hour. When demyelination occurs, however, the scar tissue sometimes slows the rate of transmission to 110 miles per hour or less. Thus, nerve impulses traveling within the brain and to the rest of the body may arrive

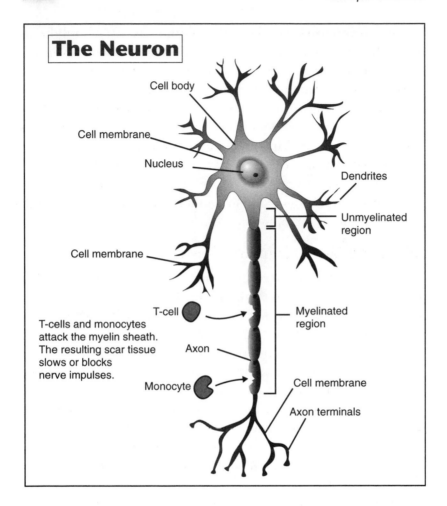

The Neuron

Cell body

Cell membrane

Nucleus

Dendrites

Unmyelinated region

Cell membrane

T-cell

T-cells and monocytes attack the myelin sheath. The resulting scar tissue slows or blocks nerve impulses.

Axon

Monocyte

Myelinated region

Cell membrane

Axon terminals

at less than half their normal speed, resulting in messages that are either garbled or ignored by other neurons.

Neurons transmit messages to other neurons by chemical signals as well as by electrical impulses. When a neuron starts an electrical impulse in response to some sort of stimulation, the current travels along the cell's axon and triggers the release of chemicals called neurotransmitters. These chemicals then travel across a small gap known as a synapse and are picked up by receptors on the dendrites of neighboring neurons.

Each cell may have hundreds or even thousands of dendrites that can receive different neurotransmitters from other neurons.

Some neurotransmitters excite the neuron, and others inhibit it. When the total amount of excitation reaches a certain level, the neuron starts its own electrical impulse, which in turn triggers it to send neurotransmitters to neighboring neurons.

There are about 100 billion neurons in a human brain, and experts estimate the number of nerve connections at about 500 trillion. Each of these 500 trillion connections can send chemical messages between one hundred and one thousand times per second. With this amount of activity involved in operating the brain, any disruptions in the speed or regularity of nerve transmission can have severe consequences.

What the Nerve Damage Does

Nerve cells in the spinal cord that regulate movement and organ function throughout the body coordinate the messages transmitted by all of the neurons and connections in the brain. Demyelination can damage neurons in any area of the brain or spinal cord, and multiple sclerosis typically begins with destruction in one location, followed by later incidents in other areas at unpredictable intervals. Depending on which areas are involved and on the size of the plaques, the affected person will show varying symptoms resulting from the breakdown—due to damaged myelin—of normal transmission of nerve impulses in those areas.

If demyelination occurs in an area of the brain known as the cerebrum, for example, memory, thinking, and sensation may be affected. Plaques in the cerebellum, the region mainly responsible for balance and movement, often lead to motion and balance difficulties. Scar tissue in the optic nerve causes vision problems. Demyelination in various areas of the spinal cord may make it impossible for instructions from the brain to get through; therefore, the person may not have control over an arm, leg, or body organ such as the bladder.

No matter what body system is affected, a demyelinating attack —that is, the appearance or worsening of symptoms for at least twenty-four hours—almost always comes on very suddenly. Indeed, says one physician who specializes in neurological diseases, "The major symptom of MS is a sudden loss of neurological function."[7] The attacks last for varying lengths of time in different people, and similar plaques can affect different individuals to varying degrees. Some patients may experience severe paralysis, but others may have only mild numbness from a particular size plaque. In still other people, a demyelinated area may heal without causing any symptoms.

In individuals in whom demyelination produces noticeable symptoms, these symptoms may lessen or go away after the inflammation from an attack is reduced and the process of repair begins. Sometimes, though, the damage is so extensive that certain symptoms linger; in some individuals, the scar tissue permanently prevents the affected nerve from transmitting impulses, even if the myelin repairs itself. Recent research has discovered that in such people the entire nerve axon, along with the protective myelin sheath, is damaged during an attack and heals only partially or not at all.

Categorizing MS Symptoms

The wide variety of plaque locations in the nervous system and the differing individual responses mean that doctors must look at a diverse range of symptoms and severity in attempting to diagnose the disease. Physicians divide the symptoms of MS into three categories. Primary symptoms are a direct result of demyelination in specific nerves; examples are numbness and loss of vision. Secondary symptoms are complications due to primary symptoms. For instance, the primary symptom of paralysis can lead to a secondary symptom of muscles wasting away due to inactivity. Tertiary symptoms are the emotional, mental, and social complications resulting from primary and secondary symptoms. For example, a patient who becomes unable to walk may lose his or her job and then fall into depression, a tertiary symptom due to job loss. Most MS patients are affected to some degree by primary, secondary, and tertiary symptoms.

Some Typical Primary Symptoms

Some of the most common early primary symptoms of MS are vision problems such as partial blindness, double vision, and fo-

Primary Symptoms of MS

Although each MS case is different, most patients experience one or more of the following primary symptoms:

- Vision problems
- Pain
- Urinary incontinence
- Weakness
- Numbness
- Tremors
- Fatigue

- Muscle spasms
- Dizziness
- Balance and coordination problems
- Paralysis
- Cognitive problems
- Depression
- Mood swings

cusing difficulties. Optic neuritis, an inflammation of the optic nerve that connects the eyes to the brain, is also common. Optic neuritis results in pain, blurring, graying, and loss of vision. Any of these vision problems can lead to permanent blindness unless promptly treated.

Pain in various places in the body is another typical primary symptom of MS. The pain can feel like a burning sensation, known as dysesthesia, or can take the form of a stabbing sensation sort of like an electric shock moving from the back of the head down the spine. The stabbing pain is called Lhermitte's sign. Another common form of pain in MS is trigeminal neuralgia, a stabbing pain in the face and jaw.

Patients say that one of the most prominent primary symptoms of MS is fatigue, particularly in hot weather. Engaging in a full day of activities or traveling someplace often intensifies this fatigue. Doug, who was diagnosed with MS at age forty-one, says, "When

I go on a trip, it takes me weeks to recover from the fatigue."[8] However, the fatigue associated with MS may have nothing to do with getting or not getting enough sleep; it can happen any time, even within an hour of awakening after a full night's rest. Affected people describe this fatigue as a heavy, dragged-down feeling that makes moving around difficult, if not impossible.

Weakness, numbness, and tremors are other commonly seen primary symptoms. Sometimes these symptoms are so severe that they prevent the individual from feeling or using a limb or other body part.

At least 80 percent of MS sufferers develop a loss of bladder control due to plaques interfering with nerve impulses telling the bladder to empty or to retain urine. This loss of control, known as urinary incontinence, can result in a frequent need to urinate and in constant leakage. It also frequently leads to the secondary symptom of bladder and urinary tract infections. In rare cases, some patients develop bowel incontinence in addition to urinary incontinence.

Additional Primary Symptoms

Dizziness, problems with balance and coordination, and muscle spasms are other primary MS symptoms that affect many patients and often lead to the secondary symptoms of not being able to walk, having trouble grasping objects, and experiencing difficulties performing simple tasks like bathing and dressing. Many people also have trouble with ordinary capabilities like swallowing, since MS can interfere with the swallowing muscles, and with speaking, due to plaques in the brain stem and cerebellum forcing the person to slur words or speak slowly.

Besides these physical problems, demyelination also commonly leads to mental and emotional difficulties ranging from thought and memory deficits to severe depression and violent mood swings. Affected persons say that these aspects of the disease are among the most terrifying since they become afraid that they are losing their mental capabilities and their sanity.

The most commonly reported cognitive, or thinking, problems are difficulties with organization, attention, concentration, learn-

A woman who has MS is wheeled into the back of her van by a home health care worker.

ing new things, and memory. Twenty-three-year-old Megan, for example, found that MS severely impacted her ability to concentrate. "I'll start talking about the things I want to do and then I'll lose track of them real easy,"[9] she explains. Experts say that about 40 percent of people with MS experience mild levels of cognitive dysfunction, and about 10 percent are affected to a moderate or severe degree by these problems.

Some patients have trouble remembering the names of objects or with putting words together into sentences, but very few encounter changes in their ability to reason or solve problems.

Doctors report that emotional problems such as depression that often accompany MS are sometimes due to demyelination in certain areas of the brain that control emotions and are thus considered primary symptoms. Other times, these emotional difficulties result from despair over having the disease or from adverse effects of medications used to treat MS and are labeled as secondary or tertiary symptoms. Either way, patients and their families consider the emotional ups and downs that affect over 50 percent of individuals with the disease to be as frustrating as the physical and mental symptoms since they are unpredictable and can erupt at any time.

Symptom Patterns

Because individuals with MS can have such a wide variety of physical, mental, and emotional symptoms, doctors must look at patterns rather than at specific complaints in making a diagnosis of MS. "The most important aspect of MS is not any single symptom: it is the way the disease acts over time," [10] explains Dr. Roger S. Cicala in *The Brain Disorders Sourcebook*.

There is no single test that can be used to diagnose MS. A doctor who suspects that a person has the disease will generally make a referral to a neurologist—a physician who specializes in disorders of the nervous system. This specialist will begin to monitor the patient's symptoms over an extended period of time. When certain patterns develop and laboratory tests are used to rule out other conditions, a diagnosis can be made. These patterns include either two separate neurological attacks at least one month apart or a progressive series of attacks over six months. The other requirement for a diagnosis of MS is a set of test results indicating more than one area of myelin damage in the central nervous system.

Given these accepted criteria for diagnosis, many months or even years may pass before a doctor can arrive at a diagnosis. Some combinations of symptoms progress very slowly, and some patients' attacks are spaced widely apart. Thirty-six-year-old Nancy, for example, experienced blurred vision in one eye. Her eye doctor found nothing wrong with the eye and sent her to a neurologist, who performed tests that revealed nothing abnormal. Nancy's vision soon returned to normal, but a year later she developed pain in her left leg. Again, the neurologist found nothing wrong. Soon afterward, however, when Nancy's right arm began burning and tingling, the doctor conducted tests that revealed evidence of nerve plaques and was finally able to reach a diagnosis of MS.

The Diagnostic Process

The first step in the diagnostic process involves the physician taking a patient history to learn about medical conditions that run in the individual's family and about when the present symptoms began. Then, the doctor performs a physical examination that includes tests of muscle strength, reflexes, coordination, and sensation. These tests help determine which parts of the nervous system may not be working correctly. One such test that is commonly done is a nerve conduction study, more frequently referred to as an evoked potential. This test measures the electrical energy that is evoked, or stimulated, by certain events in the environment. Doctors may apply electrical stimulation to the skin or use visual stimuli such as light and darkness to determine how well nerve signals are transmitted along specific nerves. The nerves of MS patients frequently conduct impulses abnormally slowly due to myelin damage, and an abnormal reading is a good indication that MS may be present.

The physician will also order blood tests that can rule out diseases like diabetes or thyroid disorders, which can cause neurological symptoms similar to those of MS. He or she may also perform an electrocardiogram to test how well the heart is working and tests of memory and thinking to further clarify the diagnosis.

Once a doctor is fairly certain that the patient's problem lies in the central nervous system, a diagnosis of MS can be confirmed by means of an MRI (magnetic resonance imaging) scan. MRI scans use a powerful magnetic field to detect chemical differences in various internal body tissues. The information is transferred to a computer, which prints pictures of the brain and spinal cord. Upon examining these images, doctors can see where nerve plaques are located and can estimate how long they have been there. Although about 5 percent of MS patients will have a normal MRI scan during the early stages of the disease, the other 95 percent will show plaques indicating MS. Based on the high percentage of cases revealed by this test, an MRI scan is currently considered to be the most accurate test for helping to diagnose MS.

A patient waits for an MRI scan, the most accurate way to test for multiple sclerosis.

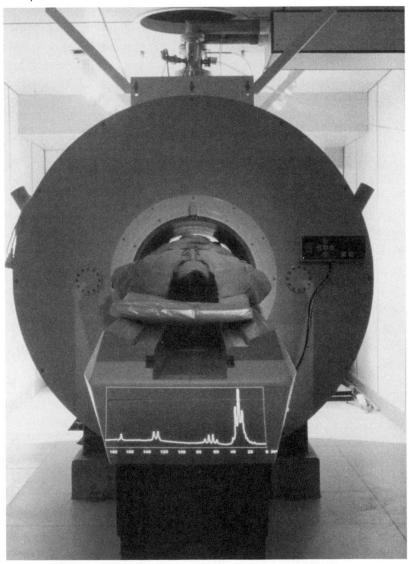

Another test that doctors frequently perform to help confirm a diagnosis of MS is a lumbar puncture, or spinal tap, to obtain cerebrospinal fluid, the clear liquid that bathes and protects the brain and spinal cord. The physician places a hollow needle between the bones of the lower back, also known as the lumbar area. The needle punctures the sack containing cerebrospinal fluid, and a small amount is withdrawn and sent to a laboratory to test for immune system proteins called oligoclonal bands. The presence of oligonclonal bands means that there is some sort of inflammation in the central nervous system. About 90 percent of people with MS have these proteins in their cerebrospinal fluid, so finding them, along with other characteristics of MS, is a fairly reliable indication that a person has this disorder.

After the Tests

Once a physician has completed the examination and laboratory tests, he or she will issue a diagnosis of "possible," "probable," or "definite" MS. A possible MS diagnosis is given when some criteria for the disease apply, but results from tests like the MRI scan are inconclusive. A probable MS diagnosis occurs when other conditions that could account for the patient's symptoms have been ruled out, but the patient has not experienced enough attacks in different areas of the nervous system to be definitely categorized as having MS. Only when the person fulfills the criteria of multiple attacks with multiple areas of demyelination indicated by an MRI scan can a diagnosis of definite MS be given.

After the Diagnosis

Although it is impossible to predict the precise course of MS for a newly diagnosed individual, the pattern of symptoms that emerges during the first five years is usually a good indication of the long-term outlook for that particular patient. For instance, people who have few attacks during the first five years generally do not experience severe disability, but those who have more frequent attacks, which include tremors and difficulties in walking, tend to fare worse in the long run.

Based on these patterns of symptoms, doctors are able to divide the disorder into four main categories. Even when a certain category seems right for a given person at a specific time, however, the course of the disease may change. Thus, being diagnosed with a particular form of MS is no guarantee that the disease will never morph into another category.

The Four Main Types of Multiple Sclerosis

The four main categories of MS are relapsing-remitting, primary-progressive, secondary-progressive, and progressive-relapsing.

The most common type of MS is the relapsing-remitting form. Seventy to 75 percent of MS patients start off with this form of the disease, in which the person experiences a sudden attack with symptoms affecting one or more areas of the body. The patient partially or fully recovers from the attack, and the disease does not progress until the next acute attack occurs. This can happen soon afterward or years later.

Primary-progressive MS is the most serious form of MS and affects about 15 percent of patients. People with the primary-

---

Types of MS

Relapsing-remitting: Sudden attack, then no progression until the next attack.

Primary-progressive: Steadily gets worse.

Secondary-progressive: Starts off with relapsing-remitting, then becomes progressive.

Progressive-relapsing: Progressive damage from the beginning, but also attacks with a remission of symptoms.

progressive type steadily worsen with little or no recovery be-tween attacks. Such patients often experience severe disability within five years of the initial symptoms.

People with secondary-progressive MS start off with the relapsing-remitting form of the disease and later switch to the progressive form. Within ten years after the disease begins, about 50 percent of the people initially diagnosed with relapsing-remitting MS are rediagnosed with the secondary-progressive form. About 90 percent of the patients who start off with relapsing-remitting MS develop secondary-progressive MS within twenty-five years.

Patients with progressive-relapsing MS, the fourth form of the disease, show progressive damage from the beginning but also experience acute attacks in which some symptoms appear and then lessen over time. This form of MS affects 6 to 10 percent of the people who have the disorder and is most commonly seen in individuals who develop MS after age forty.

In addition to these four main types of multiple sclerosis, doc-tors also refer to a mild form of the disease called the benign sen-sory form. Patients with this particular brand of MS experience attacks involving only loss of vision or other sensations. Symp-toms are usually temporary, and this type of MS rarely leads to any permanent disability, though the attacks can recur as unpre-dictably as do those in the other forms of the disease.

Chapter 2

What Causes Multiple Sclerosis?

Although doctors now have several reliable methods of diagnosing multiple sclerosis, no one has yet determined what causes the disease. Indeed, experts have been baffled about the causes of MS ever since it was first identified during the 1800s. Jean Cruveilhier, the doctor credited with first describing the disorder in 1835, believed it resulted from a patient's inability to sweat, based on the observation that heat seemed to worsen MS attacks. However, doctors now know that although heat does tend to exacerbate symptoms, sweating or not sweating neither causes MS nor protects people against it.

Jean Martin Charcot, the French neurologist who gave MS its official name, suspected the cause was related to exposure to cold, to emotional upsets, or to a previous infection with a disease like typhoid fever, cholera, or smallpox. Though exposure to cold and emotional upset are now known not to cause the disease, Charcot's idea that a previous infection might be responsible is still being tested by researchers and may indeed prove to be a critical underlying trigger.

Other Early Ideas About the Causes of MS

Other doctors who studied MS during the late 1800s and early 1900s suggested a variety of other theories about what causes the disease. Several experts believed that too much thinking was responsible; this was later proved to be incorrect. The renowned neurologist Sigmund Freud, whose ideas about the influences of the unconscious mind on physical and mental disorders ushered

Sigmund Freud attributed the development of MS to what he called "female hysteria."

in a new era of psychiatric practices, believed that what he called "female hysteria" caused MS. Scientific research, however, has since established that neither emotional problems nor thought processes have anything to do with causing multiple sclerosis.

Another line of prominent theories about MS centered on environmental toxins like lead, copper, nickel, mercury, and pesticides, but evidence has not supported a causal role for any of these factors. Other disproven biologically oriented ideas have included vitamin deficiencies, a diet high in animal fats, allergies, blood clots in the brain, a direct attack by a virus, inborn defects in the nervous system, and physical traumas such as falling. Suggestions that vaccinations cause MS, based on reports of the disease beginning soon after vaccinations for smallpox, typhoid fever, yellow fever, rabies, diphtheria, tetanus, hepatitis, and influenza have been investigated as well. So far, however, studies have not proven that any vaccination is responsible for MS, despite occasional media reports leaving the impression that such a connection has been established.

Modern Theories

Modern scientific inquiry into what causes MS has focused both on the underlying external factors that may trigger the disease and on the changes in the nervous system that cause symptoms once the process begins.

According to the National Multiple Sclerosis Society, "While the precise causes of MS are not yet known, much scientific research indicates that a number of factors in combination are probably involved."[11] The majority of MS experts now believe that these factors include the immune system, heredity, and certain environmental variables such as a previous viral infection. The geographic location where an individual lives and the influence of certain hormones in the body are also being studied as possibly contributing to the development of the disease.

The Immune System

The first evidence that the immune system played an important role in causing MS appeared in 1938, when Dr. Thomas Rivers of the Rockefeller Institute in New York demonstrated that laboratory animals' bodies would attack myelin under certain conditions and produce a disease similar to MS. The animal disease, known as experimental allergic encephalomyelitis (EAE), would later serve as the basis for many further experiments into the causes of MS in people.

More evidence on immune involvement came in 1947, when Dr. Elvin Kabat of Columbia University in New York discovered

*Dr. Thomas Rivers demonstrated that under certain conditions animals'
immune systems could produce an MS-like disease.*

that the cerebrospinal fluid of MS patients contains the abnormal immune proteins called oligoclonal bands. During the 1950s new information on how immune cells attack the substance known as MBT (myelin basic protein) lent further ammunition to the idea that an immune system problem was somehow responsible for causing MS.

In the years since these early studies were completed, doctors have accumulated even more evidence on how the immune system works and on what may go wrong with it to trigger multiple sclerosis. Experts now know that the immune system involves a complex set of cells and chemicals in the body. Some of the most important components are white blood cells, antibodies, and chemicals called cytokines that regulate the activities of immune cells.

Immune Cells Cross the Blood-Brain Barrier

White blood cells called T cells, or T lymphocytes, are believed to be the main kind of cells involved in triggering multiple sclerosis.

T cells normally circulate in the blood and travel to various places in the body to attack foreign invaders like viruses and bacteria. They usually do not enter the central nervous system because of the so-called blood-brain barrier that keeps most substances circulating in the blood from entering the brain and spinal cord. Scientists believe that this mechanism evolved to safeguard the all-important control center of the body from most of the poisons and other potentially dangerous foreign elements to which a person or animal is exposed.

In people with MS, however, T cells somehow cross the blood-brain barrier and attack the myelin in certain neurons in the central nervous system. Researchers do not yet know how or why some T cells are able to get into the brain and spinal cord, nor do they know why these cells attack the person's own myelin. Normally, T cells attack only foreign substances known as antigens, but when the T cells for some reason fail to recognize the myelin

T cells, which normally attack viruses and bacteria in the bloodstream, will attack myelin if they enter the central nervous system.

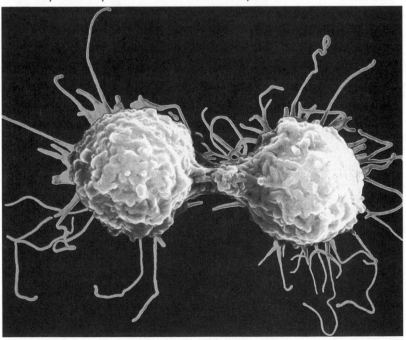

as "self," they launch an assault that subsequently causes the symptoms of MS. Such an attack on the self is called an autoimmune reaction.

Experts have discovered that three kinds of T cells all play a role in the autoimmune reaction that contributes to MS. The first kind, helper T cells, are responsible for recognizing the presence of antigens and for stimulating other white blood cells to produce antibodies—chemicals that are custom-made to neutralize specific antigens. Helper T cells also produce chemicals called cytokines, which activate other T cells to attack myelin. Laboratory tests indicate that people with MS have abnormally high numbers of helper T cells in their myelin and in the cerebrospinal fluid.

The second type of T cells, suppressor T cells, turn off the immune response that is triggered when a healthy person's system encounters an antigen. Researchers have found that MS patients have abnormally few suppressor T cells in their blood. This may prevent the person's immune system from recognizing myelin as a part of the body, thereby allowing an attack on it to proceed.

The third kind of T cells are cytotoxic, or killer, T cells. These cells directly attack and destroy antigens. Doctors find more killer T cells than normal in the cerebrospinal fluid of people with MS and believe that this increased presence, along with abnormal quantities of other types of T cells, is at least partially responsible for MS attacks and possibly for the persistence of certain symptoms caused by demyelination.

Macrophages, another kind of white blood cell that normally benefits the immune system by engulfing and destroying antigens, are also involved in the destruction of myelin. Macrophages secrete enzymes called proteases, which can destroy myelin, and prostaglandins, which cause inflammation. They also consume dead myelin after other cells have destroyed it.

An Autoimmune Disease

Even though most experts today agree that an autoimmune response is central to the development of MS, ethical considerations make it impossible to be certain that MS is or is not truly an autoimmune disease. "Actual proof of autoimmunity requires that immune system cells that react against normal body tissue and cause damage in one subject [person] be injected into a healthy subject and cause damage and disease there as well,"[12] explain the authors of *Multiple Sclerosis: A Guide for the Newly Diagnosed.*

Although studies with laboratory animals have found that the disease EAE, which is very similar to MS, is truly an autoimmune disorder, researchers obviously cannot inject healthy humans with MS patients' immune cells to see what will happen. Because of the similarities between MS and EAE, however, most modern experts believe that MS is indeed an autoimmune disease.

The Role of Genes

Although scientists have not proven exactly what causes the autoimmune reaction that underlies MS, recent evidence points to a necessary genetic component. Genes are the parts of a DNA (deoxyribonucleic acid) molecule that pass hereditary information from parents to their offspring. They are found in the center of each human cell on wormlike bodies called chromosomes. The sequence of genes on each DNA molecule encodes a particular set of instructions telling the cell what to do.

Genetic information can either be passed directly or inherited as a predisposition. Examples of directly transmitted genetic traits are hair color and eye color; such traits appear in the offspring at birth regardless of environmental or biological events. In contrast, a genetic predisposition is an inherited tendency to develop a particular trait. However, unless certain additional factors are present, the person is not likely to show that trait.

Experts believe that a genetic predisposition is involved in the development of multiple sclerosis. That is, people who get MS probably are born with an inherited tendency toward the disorder. Those who inherit this tendency seem not to get the disease, however, unless certain triggering environmental events are present.

Studies indicate that some environmental events cause DNA damage that later prompts the affected person's body to launch an autoimmune attack on myelin. Damage to genes and chromosomes from changes in the base chemicals that form DNA are known as mutations. Although some mutations are passed to an

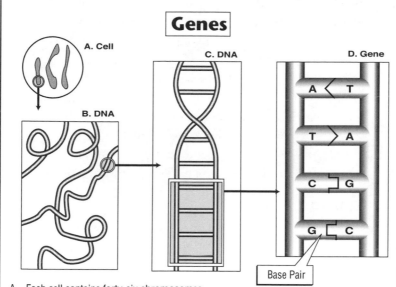

Genes

A. Cell

B. DNA

C. DNA

D. Gene

A < T

T > A

C G

G C

Base Pair

A. Each cell contains forty-six chromosomes.

B. A chromosome is a chainlike strand of DNA.

C. When the chromosome is greatly magnified under a microscope, it looks like a long ladder that is twisted into a double helix. The twisting allows these amazingly long strands to fit inside a single tiny cell.

D. The rungs of the DNA ladder are made up of the four base pairs—AT, TA, GC, and CG. The letters stand for the four bases that make up the pairs: adenine, guanine, cytosine, and thymine. Each sequence of base pairs that contains the instructions for making a single protein is called a gene.

offspring directly through the parents' egg and sperm cells, such changes also can result from damage to the cells that occurs during an individual's lifetime. In the case of MS, experts believe DNA damage from an event during the early life of a person having a genetic predisposition for MS results in the development of the disease many years later.

Evidence for a Genetic Link

Researchers are currently investigating the exact role that genes and a genetic predisposition play in causing MS. One avenue of research that supports the theory that an inherited susceptibility is critical involves the study of families in which the disease appears

*Having a family history of MS greatly increases the chances
of getting the disease.*

again and again. Scientists have discovered that having a family
history of MS significantly increases the risk of getting the disease.
Children who have a parent with MS have about a 3 percent
chance of developing MS themselves, whereas the risk in the general population is one-tenth of 1 percent. Identical twins, who have
identical sets of genes, carry an even greater risk. If one twin develops MS, the other has about a 10 percent chance of getting the
disease, indicating that a genetic susceptibility plays a strong role.

Other evidence for a genetic influence in causing MS comes
from studies showing that the disorder is more common among
Caucasians than among other races, even when different racial
groups live in the same geographic area. For example, Canadian
Caucasians get MS more frequently than other Canadians do,
whereas Eskimos living in Canada rarely develop the disease. In
a similar manner, certain racial and ethnic groups that, like the

Eskimos, tend to intermarry among themselves, also seem to be protected against MS. These genetically isolated groups include the Gypsies in eastern Europe and the Hutterites in Canada.

Research made possible by sophisticated modern techniques for examining genes and chromosomes has shed further light on the role of genetic factors in causing MS. By analyzing DNA with equipment such as electron microscopes and chromatographs, which allow visualization of the different components of DNA, scientists have identified certain recognizable patterns of genes in people with a particular disease. These patterns, known as genetic markers, may prove to be important in predicting who is susceptible to developing these disorders. Several recent studies have shown, for example, that people who have a genetic marker for a certain white blood cell antigen are very likely to develop MS.

The discovery of a specific genetic indicator of a predisposition to MS is grounds for suspecting that the abnormality represented by this marker may be at least partly responsible for causing the disease. Further research is trying to identify other genetic markers characteristic of MS patients in the hopes of pinpointing a gene or genes responsible for the illness. As many as twenty different genes have been implicated to date.

Environmental Events

Along with a genetic predisposition and at least one autoimmune attack, modern experts believe that one or more environmental events are essential in causing MS. Evidence indicates that one of the primary environmental culprits is some sort of virus.

Doctors have suspected that viruses might be involved in MS since the early 1900s. One of the first physicians to postulate a viral link was W.E. Bullock, who in 1913 reported having transmitted MS from humans to rabbits and guinea pigs by injecting the animals with cerebrospinal fluid from multiple sclerosis patients. Bullock believed that the cerebrospinal fluid contained a virus that was responsible for the MS. Other researchers later claimed to have achieved the same result, but no one, including Bullock, was able to prove that any virus or other infectious agent was involved. More recent studies also failed to confirm the finding that MS could be transmitted from people to animals, and experts have since determined that the disease is not contagious to either animals or people.

However, even though medical science has established that MS is not caused directly by an active viral infection, increasing evidence points to an important role for an infection received earlier, perhaps years before the onset of MS. People with MS have antibodies against certain viruses in their cerebrospinal fluid, and this finding has led researchers to try to determine which of many viruses might be involved in triggering the disease long after the actual infection took place.

Which Viruses?

"Many viruses and pathogens have been associated with MS, although none has been tightly linked to disease,"[13] says researcher Donald H. Gilden of the University of Colorado Health Sciences Center in Denver.

Scientists have investigated whether viruses as diverse as measles, mumps, canine distemper, rabies, influenza, hepatitis, herpes, and Epstein-Barr play a role in MS. Many MS patients have antibodies to one or more of these viruses, but so far there has been no proof that a previous infection with any of them triggers the autoimmune destruction of myelin.

The evidence linking some of these viruses to MS goes beyond merely finding antibodies in the cerebrospinal fluid of people with the disease, but again nothing has been proven. For example, evidence that the canine distemper virus may be involved in the development of multiple sclerosis comes from a study in the Orkney Islands off the coast of Scotland. This study found that the incidence of multiple sclerosis among natives increased dramatically several years after soldiers brought their dogs to these islands during World War II. When the dog population declined, the rate of MS dropped too. The investigators who conducted the study claimed that most likely the canine distemper virus was responsible, but scientists who have analyzed the same data point out that a direct link between the canine virus and MS was not conclusively demonstrated.

Other experts have suggested that perhaps it was exposure to animals with rabies that triggered these cases of multiple sclerosis; in fact, a group of Russian scientists produced an experimental rabies virus vaccine against MS during the 1950s based on this assumption. However, the vaccine proved ineffective.

More recently, a group of researchers discovered that the human herpes virus-6 (HHV-6), which causes roseola, a disease similar to measles, appears in demyelinated areas of the brain when patients are experiencing an MS attack. Since, however, the researchers have not shown that this virus actually causes the attacks, further studies are being undertaken.

During the 1990s many French people developed MS after receiving the hepatitis B vaccine, and rumors began flying that either the vaccine or the hepatitis B virus itself caused the disease. Doctors at the Harvard University Medical School in Boston, Massachusetts, began a scientific study to test whether this was true. In February 2001 these investigators reported that hundreds of nurses who received the hepatitis B vaccine did not develop

Fears that the hepatitis B vaccine pictured here somehow causes MS have been shown to be unfounded.

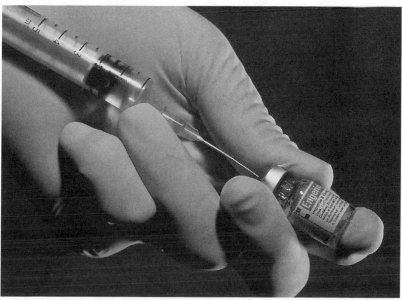

MS any more frequently than an equal number of nurses who did not receive the vaccine. Based on this research, experts have come to a consensus that the attenuated virus in the hepatitis B vaccine is probably not responsible for causing MS. Whether the live virus plays a role has yet to be determined.

In January 2002 another possible MS-related virus was reported by Dr. Alberto Ascherio and his colleagues at the Harvard School of Public Health in Boston, Massachusetts. The researchers found antibodies to the Epstein-Barr virus, which causes mononucleosis and other diseases, in the blood of a large number of people who have MS. Although further studies are needed to establish whether a previous infection with the Epstein-Barr virus can actually cause multiple sclerosis, the investigators have concluded that their research offers evidence that such an infection increases the risk of MS. However, they point out that since "few individuals infected with EBV [Epstein-Barr Virus] develop MS, other cofactors are required. These may include

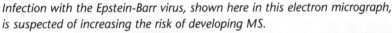

Infection with the Epstein-Barr virus, shown here in this electron micrograph, is suspected of increasing the risk of developing MS.

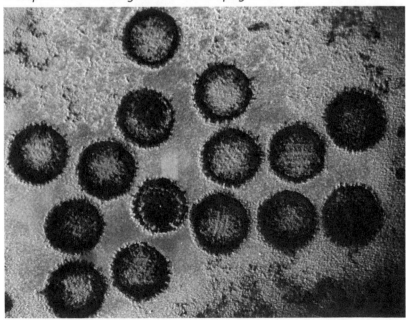

genetic predisposition and, perhaps, age at primary infection or infection with other microbes."[14]

Still a Puzzle

Although experts have not yet proven which, if any, viruses are responsible for MS, the vast amount of recent research on the topic has spawned new insights into how such an infectious agent is likely to trigger the disorder in conjunction with other factors, such as a genetic tendency. One recent theory is that perhaps whichever viruses are involved contain chemicals similar to myelin. Once the immune system produces antibodies against these viruses, the antibodies mistakenly identify the myelin itself as foreign and attack it, too, in susceptible individuals.

Another idea is that a particular viral infection disables the immune system so that it is unable to tell the difference between its own myelin and foreign substances. A similar line of reasoning proposes that one virus may attack the immune system, leaving it unable to withstand a later assault by a different, as yet unidentified, virus that triggers MS.

Modern attempts to unravel the mystery of how certain viruses and other variables cause multiple sclerosis are also examining how geographic location and the timing of an infection might interact with a genetic predisposition to trigger the disease. Since it is a well-known fact that MS occurs most often in countries farthest from the equator and in the northern parts of the United States, researchers are focusing on common viruses in these areas that may play a role. They have discovered that a person's risk of getting MS is determined by where they live up to age fifteen. Someone who lives in Michigan, for example, until age fifteen and then moves to Texas will always carry a higher risk of developing MS than will people who grow up in southern areas of the country. Many experts believe that the critical factor here may be exposure during childhood to a particular virus common in high latitudes.

The fact that most people who develop MS first show symptoms between the ages of fifteen and forty-five also suggests that the hormones that become active at puberty may play a role in

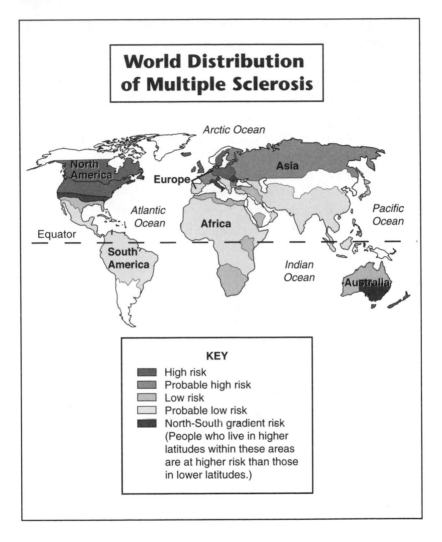

triggering the disease. This possibility has gained credence through recent studies showing that administering certain sex hormones to MS patients seems to help control attacks in many individuals with relapsing-remitting MS. Additional research showing that women with MS tend to experience fewer acute flareups of symptoms while they are pregnant indicates that perhaps the high levels of the hormones estrogen and progesterone present during pregnancy have something to do with discouraging the immune system from attacking the individual's myelin.

With so many factors involved, the struggle to clearly define the causes of MS is likely to continue for many years. However, new advances in studying how genetics, the immune system, and environmental influences interact are moving doctors closer than ever to understanding why people get the disease. In turn, this knowledge is being used to explore ways of possibly preventing MS and to develop new and more effective methods of treating this disabling disorder.

Chapter 3

How Is Multiple Sclerosis Treated?

Although there is presently no cure for multiple sclerosis, modern research has developed several medications and other treatments that slow the course of the disease and help patients cope with its symptoms. Only during the past couple of decades, however, have doctors been able to offer people with MS treatments based on good science. Prior to this time, attempted treatments based on erroneous theories had produced treatments that worked at random, if at all, and lack of knowledge about the underlying biological changes that trigger the disease had constantly thwarted efforts to help patients.

Early Treatment Attempts

During the late 1800s Jean Martin Charcot and other neurologists tried to treat MS with electric shocks and strychnine, a poison that stimulates nerves. Charcot believed that patients' symptoms would go away if their nerves were induced to conduct impulses faster through these methods. Charcot also injected gold and silver into people with MS since such injections seemed to be beneficial in the treatment of syphilis, a venereal disease characterized, in its late stages, by pronounced neurological symptoms. However, none of Charcot's treatments were effective.

Other doctors around this time tried treating MS with herbs and bed rest, but these measures neither cured the disease nor stopped the attacks. The life expectancy for an MS patient during the late 1800s was about five years after the disease began.

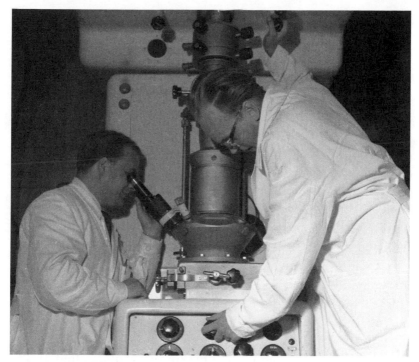

Two doctors use a microscope to examine multiple sclerosis bacteria, an example of an erroneous theory that did not lead to an effective treatment, at the University Clinic for Nervous Disease at Vienna in 1956.

During the 1930s and 1940s, physicians who wrongly believed that blood clots or impaired blood flow caused MS tried using blood thinners like dicoumarol to dissolve these clots. These drugs did nothing to prevent acute attacks or slow the progression of MS. More recently, the use of another blood thinner, heparin, was also found to be ineffective.

During the 1950s several doctors tried giving MS patients blood transfusions, theorizing that new blood might confer immunity to disease-causing viruses. Some doctors believed a transfusion would also dilute any abnormal chemicals in the person's blood that were responsible for the disorder. Transfusions, however, proved to be no more effective than doing nothing.

Many physicians tried a variety of drugs to treat MS during the 1950s in hopes of making headway against this baffling disease.

Succinates, which improve the oxygen supply in the body; tetrae-thylammonium, a blood circulation enhancer; histamine and other allergy drugs; blood pressure drugs; antidepressants; acne drugs; and various vitamin derivatives were among the many that researchers tested. Although some patients did experience a lessening of symptoms after taking one or more of these compounds, scientific studies later showed that such results were most likely due to chance since none of these drugs were truly effective against MS.

Steps in the Right Direction

During the 1960s, when researchers began to gain a clearer understanding of the role of the immune system in MS, doctors began to test cortisone and related compounds that suppress inflammation in the body. When it was discovered that giving animals the steroidal hormone ACTH could prevent them from getting the MS-like disease experimental allergic encephalo-myelitis (EAE), investigators decided to try this substance on humans with multiple sclerosis. A 1969 study concluded that ACTH was the first-ever drug to speed the recovery of acute MS flare-ups, and soon the use of various steroids to treat acute attacks became standard medical practice.

Steroids shorten acute MS attacks by reducing inflammation in the nervous system, but they do not help prevent relapses or slow the overall progression of the disease. It was not until the 1980s that researchers began to make headway in developing drugs that would actually slow the progression of MS. Most disease-slowing medications regulate the immune system using man-made copies of chemicals called interferons, the cytokines produced by the immune system in response to antigens. A very new alternative method of inhibiting the progression of MS uses a protein similar to myelin that fools the patient's immune system into attacking the drug instead of its own myelin.

Current medical treatment of MS usually includes one or more of these disease-slowing medications, steroidal drugs to lessen the severity of sudden attacks, and still other drugs that reduce the symptoms from previous demyelinating episodes.

Drugs That Slow the Progression of MS

The synthetic interferons used to slow the progression of MS are proprietary forms of interferon beta and interferon beta 1-a. Betaseron and Betaferon, different brand names for interferon beta, have only been available since 1994, so doctors do not yet know what the long-term effects will be. But clinical studies show the drug does reduce the frequency and severity of MS attacks in about two-thirds of the people who take it. It also reduces the number of new areas of demyelination as revealed by MRI scans.

A lab worker extracts interferon beta from a glass vial. Interferon beta has been shown to slow the development of MS.

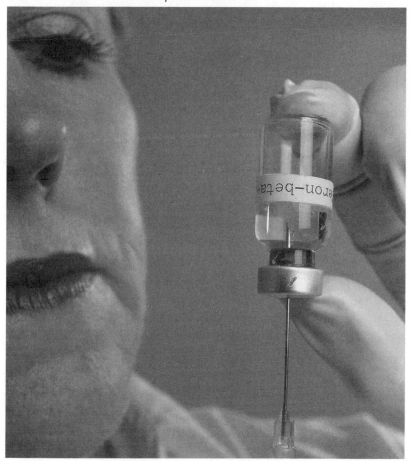

Interferon beta seems to work well on relapsing-remitting and secondary-progressive MS. It is given by injection every other day. Some patients learn to inject themselves, but others rely on a family member or other assistant. The drug causes some swelling, redness, and pain at the site of injection. It can also cause flulike symptoms, depression, and birth defects if taken by pregnant women.

The second medication used for slowing the course of MS, interferon beta 1-a, was released in 1997 and is marketed as Avonex. It is chemically more similar to naturally produced interferon than are Betaseron and Betaferon. In addition, Avonex is more convenient for patients since it must be injected only once a week rather than every other day, and in most people it does not cause as much inflammation at the injection site. Like Betaseron and Betaferon, though, Avonex often produces flulike symptoms, depression, and should not be taken during pregnancy.

Avonex works in much the same manner as Betaseron and Betaferon, reducing the severity and frequency of new MS attacks, cutting the number of nerve plaques, and allowing patients to maintain their existing level of physical and mental functioning for longer.

In 2002 the Food and Drug Administration (FDA) approved Rebif, another form of interferon beta 1-a similar to Avonex. Rebif has similar benefits and works better than Avonex in some people. Not all patients can tolerate Rebif, however, because adverse effects like inflammation at the injection site, liver problems, and reduced white blood cell count can be strong enough to rule out the use of this drug.

Glatamier acetate, marketed as Copaxone, is the other widely used disease-slowing drug available. It blocks the autoimmune destruction of myelin by acting as a decoy: Chemically similar to myelin, the drug tricks the immune system into attacking it. Since Copaxone is very new, doctors do not know how well it will work over time, but so far it appears to reduce the frequency and severity of acute attacks in people with relapsing-remitting MS. Although it does not help as high a percentage of patients as does interferon beta and must be given daily by injection, Copaxone has fewer unpleasant effects and is therefore an option for people who cannot tolerate interferon beta.

Other Options for Slowing Progression

Besides the drugs routinely used to slow the progression of MS, physicians are now able to prescribe mitoxantrone, brand name Novantrone. Originally employed for treating cancer, Novantrone recently received FDA approval as a treatment for MS. Clinical tests showed that when given intravenously once every three months it slowed the course of relapsing-remitting, secondary-progressive, and progressive-relapsing MS and reduced the number of new nerve plaques. However, the drug has many adverse effects, including nausea and hair loss, and can lead to heart and liver failure, so it must be used sparingly and is only recommended for patients who do not respond well to other treatments.

Another option for severely ill patients who do not benefit from other MS treatments is immunosuppressive drugs like closporine, normally used to prevent tissue rejection in people who receive organ transplants. With MS, these medications are only used in desperate cases since they sometimes help but sometimes create overwhelming adverse effects that make the person sicker.

The Timing of Disease-Slowing Treatment

Whichever disease-slowing drugs are chosen for a particular patient, the Medical Advisory Board of the National Multiple Sclerosis Society (NMSS) recommends that the individual begins such treatment immediately, regardless of the severity of symptoms or the frequency of relapses. The National Multiple Sclerosis Society has made it a priority to educate medical professionals about this issue since many doctors who do not specialize in MS are not aware of the need to quickly begin therapy and are inclined to wait to see if symptoms worsen. According to an NMSS publication on early intervention,

> One of the current difficulties is low referral by physicians to MS specialists for initiation of disease-modifying therapy. This

is of particular concern in light of numerous studies . . . confirming that axonal damage is coincident with destruction of the myelin sheath in the MS disease process, suggesting that even early relapses that appear benign [harmless] may have permanent neurological consequences. . . . These findings strengthen the argument for early intervention with a disease-modifying agent.[15]

In addition to quickly beginning treatment to slow the progression of the disease, experts also recommend that this therapy be continued indefinitely unless it clearly is not helping a particular patient or is producing intolerable adverse effects. "Cessation of treatment may result in a resumption of pre-treatment disease activity with serious long-term consequences,"[16] says the National Multiple Sclerosis Society.

Even with this advice, however, many patients stop taking these drugs because of unpleasant effects; refusal of medical insurance companies to cover the costs, which can be thousands of dollars per month; or due to the mistaken belief that no further nerve damage will occur until the next relapse. In light of recent MRI studies showing that even patients who seem to be in remission are actually experiencing ongoing demyelination, specialists and patient advocacy groups are working tirelessly to educate people who have MS, as well as medical professionals, about the importance of continuing treatment on a regular basis. These groups are also lobbying the federal government to require insurance companies to cover the costs of MS treatments that offer affected people a good chance of slowing their disease progression.

Treatments for Acute MS Attacks

In contrast to the recommended ongoing medications that slow the course of MS, acute flareups in the relapsing-remitting and progressive-relapsing forms of the disease call for short-term treatment with drugs of other types. Corticosteroids like prednisone and dexamethasone have remained the most commonly used compounds for this purpose since they were first investigated in the 1960s. Usually a doctor will administer large doses

Corticosteroids such as these often help reduce the severity and duration of an attack.

intravenously for four days followed by smaller doses by mouth for two to four weeks. The drugs often reduce the severity and duration of the attack; however, they cannot be used for too long because they impair the immune system and leave the patient vulnerable to infection. They also interfere with sugar metabolism, worsening or even triggering diabetes, and they cause weight gain and fluid retention. In addition, these medications can cause stomach ulcers, mood swings, fatigue, and birth defects if taken during pregnancy.

Steroids often work well in alleviating acute MS attacks that occur in the early stages of the disease, but these powerful medications are considerably less effective for patients whose diagnosis is not recent.

Some physicians are starting to use corticosteroids to treat primary-progressive MS. This is because some primary-progressive patients who steadily get worse rather than having flareups and periods of recovery may respond well to a large dose of these drugs when they are given once a month.

Treatments for Managing Symptoms from MS Attacks

Drug therapy for MS also must attempt to help patients cope with specific symptoms from past or present attacks. People who experience disabling numbness and tingling or with burning pain, for example, are often given antiseizure drugs like carba-mazepine or antidepressants like amitriptyline. Tremors and uncontrollable shaking can be treated with tranquilizers like al-prazolam; severe muscle spasms are often helped by the muscle relaxer baclofen or the sedative diazepam, commonly marketed as Valium. People with chronic spasms that are not controlled by these oral medications may get a baclofen pump surgically im-planted into the spinal cord. Sometimes doctors inject small amounts of Botox, a form of the botulinum toxin that paralyzes muscles, into small groups of spastic muscles. This treatment lasts for weeks or even months and is most effective when only one or two muscles are involved.

The many MS patients affected by bladder control problems can be treated with anticholinergic drugs that block the neuro-transmitter acetylcholine or with a blood pressure medicine called terazosin. Certain antidepressants also seem to help this problem. In fact, the antidepressant drugs prescribed to help many MS patients cope with the depression that often goes along with the disease sometimes relieve muscle spasms as well.

Patients with extreme fatigue may be given Ritalin, a central nervous system stimulant commonly used to treat attention deficit hyperactivity disorder. This drug also causes loss of appetite and addiction, however, and many people prefer not to take it.

Complementary Treatments

Drugs used to treat the symptoms and progression of multiple sclerosis are not the only forms of therapy needed in most cases. Many patients also require physical therapy, occupational ther-apy, speech therapy, and psychological counseling as well. These forms of treatment are all known as complementary therapies since they complement, or work to enhance, the benefits provided by medication. Sometimes they are referred to as rehabilitation therapies.

Physical therapy is performed by a licensed physical therapist to help certain body parts function as well as possible during sudden MS attacks and after an attack has caused some sort of disability. When an acute attack causes paralysis, for example, physical therapy that involves stretching and massage helps prevent permanent shortening of the muscles and helps reduce muscle spasms. After an attack, physical therapy is used to retrain muscles so they can work again. The therapist prescribes certain exercises and often uses electrical stimulation to increase strength and movement ability. Some patients may have to learn to walk again or to use other muscle groups that were temporarily disabled.

Physical therapists also fit patients for necessary assistance devices such as leg braces, walkers, canes, splints, and wheelchairs. Although such devices are sold without prescriptions in many retail outlets, experts recommend that individuals seek professional help in selection and fitting. Discomfort or even infection can result from improperly fitted equipment.

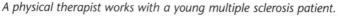

A physical therapist works with a young multiple sclerosis patient.

Occupational Therapy

Occupational therapists work with patients to correct specific problems with everyday tasks. Carol, for instance, was having trouble dressing because of extreme weakness in one hand and one leg, so an occupational therapist suggested she purchase a dressing stick, sock pullers, special buttonhooks, and a zipper puller. Such tools are available through health aid stores and are of enormous benefit to patients who have trouble bending, reaching, or stepping into clothing or shoes. The therapist also suggested that Carol sit while dressing and buy shoes with velcro tabs instead of laces.

Occupational therapists often recommend other tools, including special pen and pencil grips, special combs and brushes, and special nail clippers. Sometimes they advise making structural changes to a home or workplace to accommodate a patient's needs. Many patients with dizziness or weakness benefit from special toilets, grab bars and safety rails for the bathroom, and tub chairs. Others require the installation of wheelchair ramps or modified doorways to accommodate scooters or wheelchairs.

For people with urinary incontinence, an occupational therapist will often work with a medical doctor to help the person decide on a method of dealing with this problem. Even people who take medication for incontinence find the drugs do not entirely take care of the issue. Some patients use diapers to deal with the leakage of urine, but others prefer a catheter, which is a thin plastic or rubber tube with an attached plastic bag. The tube is inserted through the urethra into the bladder, where it collects urine. The bag is emptied when full. For many patients, a catheter is uncomfortable and emotionally devastating since it signifies a lack of control, but many learn to accept it as an unpleasant necessity.

Speech Therapy

Many people with MS require speech therapy because nerve plaques impair normal speech and make them slur their words or take long pauses between words. Speech therapists evaluate the specific problem and help the person learn to speak in a way that is easier to understand. New ways of breathing and enunciating often must be introduced. Speech therapists can also help patients who have swallowing difficulties. Special exercises and dietary changes are usually enough to allow the individual to swallow in a satisfactory manner. If the person is unable to swallow any food, however, a feeding tube is inserted to give adequate nutrition.

Psychological Counseling

Difficulties in coping with a disease like MS often lead to depression and other forms of psychological malfunctions. In addition, many patients also experience emotional problems as a result of demyelination in certain areas of the brain. It is therefore very common for people with MS to need psychotherapy as well as various medications that help them deal with these aspects of the disease.

Many different forms of psychotherapy can be beneficial. All involve the patient talking about his or her anxieties with a licensed therapist, who then can recommend changes in thinking or behavior designed to alleviate the emotional distress.

Alternative Therapy

Even with the many drug and complementary therapies available to MS patients, most still experience varying degrees of disability and pain. Desperate for anything that might help, and always aware that none of these treatments actually cure the disease, many people try alternative remedies in the hope of happening on an extraordinary discovery. In an article for the International MS Support Foundation, Dr. Randall Schapiro points out that most of the alternative treatments that are advertised in the media, particularly those claiming to be miraculous cures, have no scientific rationale and eventually prove to be of no benefit. Schapiro warns MS patients that they may be especially vulnerable to wasting time and money on such treatments because the disease is so unpredictable, frustrating, and presently incurable. Many patients, he says, are sitting on the edge of their chairs waiting for a miraculous cure to be discovered. This means that a large number of people are susceptible to sometimes dangerous forms of quackery-type medicine. When an MS patient reads about a new form of treatment, it is important for the patient to check that treatment with his or her neurologist before hopes are raised. [17]

Such treatments may include dietary changes, herbs, and food supplements, along with alternative therapies like yoga, acupuncture, chiropractic, hypnosis, aromatherapy, homeopathy, reflexology, and others. Experts say most of these are safe and not likely to do a patient any harm, though some can be detrimental if administered by an uncredentialed or fraudulent practitioner. This is why doctors recommend that patients considering any of

Doctors recommend that people with MS consult their physicians before experimenting with alternative treatments such as acupuncture.

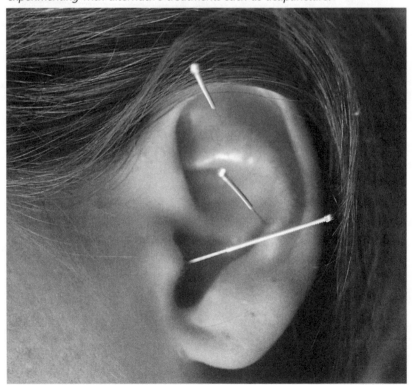

these alternatives consult their physician before proceeding. The National Multiple Sclerosis Society also keeps a database on purported remedies that are unsafe or fraudulent. The NMSS emphasizes that any claims of secret or miracle treatments should be viewed with skepticism since proven remedies are not kept secret and are available to everyone.

Some forms of alternative medicine, such as acupuncture, have been scientifically proven to help alleviate pain and some of the other symptoms of MS, and doctors have few qualms about advising individuals to add such therapies to their medical plans. Other measures, such as dietary changes, are not proven to be beneficial but are usually harmless. Diets that are free of animal fats, wheat, or sugar, for example, are among those that some MS patients claim have improved their condition, but so far no scientific evidence supports these claims. However, if an individual feels better after switching his or her eating habits, doctors say it is fine to continue with such a regimen as long as the diet is well balanced and provides essential nutrients.

Experts also caution that a patient should not discontinue his or her prescribed medications in the belief that they will be adequately helped or even cured by an alternative procedure. "Adding an alternative therapy to your medical regimen may help and will rarely cause harm. Stopping your medical therapy to try an alternative treatment may allow the disease to progress more rapidly,"[18] says Dr. Roger S. Cicala in *The Brain Disorders Sourcebook.*

A Continuing Saga

Until medical science develops treatments that are free of unpleasant effects and that provide appreciable relief for all people with MS, patients will undoubtedly continue to seek alternative methods of making their lives more tolerable. Although current conventional therapies represent significant progress over the hit-and-miss strategies that formed the medical arsenal prior to the late 1960s, experts and patients agree that there is still much work to be done before multiple sclerosis treatments allow affected people to lead truly normal lives.

Chapter 4

Living with Multiple Sclerosis

No matter how well MS treatments work for a particular individual, patients, families, and experts agree that living with the disease can be challenging, frustrating, and physically and emotionally painful from the moment of diagnosis. Even moderately serious cases interfere with nearly every aspect of life, including walking, seeing, working, playing, driving a car, and interacting with family and friends. Seriously ill young people may not be able to complete their education, embark on a career, or even leave their parents' home. MS patients who have spouses and children of their own may have to totally rearrange all aspects of childcare, work, and other activities and plans for the future.

The Impact of Diagnosis

Receiving a diagnosis of multiple sclerosis means that patients and families must suddenly adjust to living with a chronic, disabling, and entirely unpredictable illness. "Being diagnosed with MS hits you like a truck coming from the left lane: unexpectedly, even if it comes after years of wondering why your body keeps misbehaving,"[19] says an article in the National Multiple Sclerosis Society's *Inside MS*.

People respond differently to the stress of diagnosis. Some feel sorry for themselves, lash out in anger, are overwhelmed by fear, or become severely depressed with the realization that a serious illness will be a part of their identities as long as they live. "Chronic illness forces each person to confront the frailty and

60

vulnerability of the human condition in a personal and immediate way. This process involved grieving for one's former self-image and integrating the realities of MS into one's identity,"[20] explain the authors of *Multiple Sclerosis: A Guide for the Newly Diagnosed.* Families, as well as the patients themselves, also experience grief over the loss of a part of their lives.

The process of redefining one's identity calls for dealing with the reactions of other people to disability and chronic illness. Pity, discomfort, and even loathing are frequent reactions that a patient encounters from both family and other people. Often family members become impatient with the person with MS because many of the symptoms, such as blurred vision and pain, are invisible and the patient may seem to be imagining that something is wrong. Other times, the cognitive changes MS produces may lead to difficulties in conversing, remembering names, or organizing appointments and chores. Those who do

MS patients often find themselves isolated because of their inability to move around easily.

not understand the ramifications of the disease, whether family members or people the patient encounters in social and employment-related situations, may resent these failings. Their resentment, in turn, can cause the patient to lash out and further alienate those around him or her.

Sometimes the stresses associated with adjusting to a diagnosis of MS are so overwhelming that people deny the illness is really happening. For example, Lisa, a young woman with MS, says, "It was probably a good year before I even started to accept the fact that I have MS. There was no way I could have it—I'm too active and do so many things."[21] Experts point out, however, that denial is not useful in adjusting to the disease; indeed, it can be dangerous if it prevents someone from starting necessary treatment.

Other patients feel relieved after diagnosis. For many people, just having a label for what is wrong with them is more comforting than endless wondering over what they are facing. Some who have gone from doctor to doctor without receiving a definitive diagnosis say that actually finding out that they have MS is oddly a relief.

After Diagnosis

Whether individuals and families are primarily relieved, frightened, or depressed over a diagnosis of MS, mental health authorities find that those who work through the grieving process without trying to deny what is happening eventually end up with the strength to do what is necessary to cope. "Learning that you have MS is a bitter pill, especially if the symptoms cause dramatic changes in your body and in your lifestyle. So go ahead and mourn. But after you've mourned and processed it through to the best of your ability, let it go and determine to make the best of what fate has handed you,"[22] advise MS experts David L. Carroll and Jon Dudley Dorman.

Even those patients who manage to make the best of their situation, however, often need counseling and antidepressant medication to help them deal with the daily frustrations. Over half of all people with MS experience major depression sometime during the course of the illness. Although many overcome this depression with appropriate therapy, others never climb out of a state of despair. Says one woman who could not put her anger and depression aside, "Every morning when I wake up and realize my legs don't work right I go through a kind of mini-anger tantrum deep inside myself. It happens every day like clockwork."[23]

Making the Best of Living with MS

Doctors and MS support and advocacy groups make every effort to help patients deal constructively with negative emotions and

An MS patient sits before his computer, playing virtual golf. Keeping a positive attitude is a key factor in coping with the challenges of the disease.

MS patients participate in exercises to increase upper body conditioning. Regular exercise can help people with MS lead healthier lives.

lead productive lives. Many people find that, once they can express their concerns and receive concrete suggestions for coping, they are able to accept the challenges of living with MS as each presents itself.

Developing a positive attitude is a key factor in adjusting to life with MS. According to affected patients and MS experts, essential elements in such an attitude include accepting the limitations MS may place on activities while striving to do whatever is possible, maintaining a sense of humor, making the most of each day, and vowing not to give up.

Lisa offers one example of how a positive attitude can influence the quality of life with a chronic, incurable condition:

> If I had never had MS, I would never have traveled the way I did. I took a year off after I was diagnosed and traveled all around Europe. I decided I was going to do things while I could because I didn't know when something might be taken

away from me. And I think one thing I've learned from MS is to do things while I can. It's a lesson for everyone. We should all live each day to the fullest, because we never know when something might happen to take it away.[24]

Doug, who has severe primary-progressive MS with substantial disabilities, has also managed to make the best of his condition and focus on the positives in his life. "This disease is terrible, but it has been a blessing because it has brought wonderful people into my life who would not have been there otherwise," he says. "It's also given me the opportunity to help others—I counsel other people with MS and help them lobby their insurance companies or the government so they can get the treatments they need."[25]

Like Doug, many people with MS find that helping others adds meaning to their lives and significantly reduces the amount of time they spend worrying about their condition. Other tried-and-true methods for promoting a positive attitude are cultivating religious or spiritual beliefs, doing yoga or engaging in similar modes of relaxation, and developing or maintaining hobbies of interest. According to Carroll and Dorman,

> Time and time again health care professionals have witnessed that MS persons who are committed to something higher—be this a religious belief, a meditation practice, or a simple unselfish interest in service and placing others' needs before their own—are often those who thrive best, the ones who remain most healthy, most active, most content.[26]

Although a positive attitude and a dedication to certain activities can make living with MS easier, physicians point out that nothing will enable an individual to control flareups or stabilize the course of the disease. Some people believe that their MS will not get worse if they focus their energies on fighting it, but experts warn that this is not a realistic expectation. Such individuals often feel they have failed when their condition worsens or when they must finally depend on a wheelchair or other assistance device. However, those who manage to maintain a positive attitude learn to view the wheelchair as a vehicle that enables them to enjoy an afternoon in the park rather than as a despised crutch that represents their failure to recover the use of their legs.

Taking Control

Patient advocates find that part of the reason a positive attitude has such a strong influence on the quality of life with MS is that it is the first step toward achieving a degree of control in a most difficult situation. Once a person moves ahead with a positive attitude, he or she can then take additional steps that promote a further degree of control.

Many patients find that one important aspect of taking control is getting organized. Making lists of daily chores and obligations, carefully assigning priorities to different jobs, and making accomodations for not-so-good days are specific organizational skills that can help in adjusting to life with MS.

Another important way of taking charge is learning about the disease: asking questions, reading books, exploring MS websites, and joining organizations like the National Multiple Sclerosis Society that provide information and support. Educated patients and families who understand how the disease may progress, what treatments are available, and what measures they can take to stay as healthy as possible are better able to make decisions concerning lifestyle changes and other issues the disease presents.

Also important in taking control is choosing a good health care provider. Since most people with MS live for a long time with the disease, this decision affects long-term care and management. Experts say the physician should be a well-qualified neurologist who is experienced in treating MS. Personal attributes such as compassion and a willingness to provide detailed information are also important. The patient should feel like the doctor is concerned enough to fully evaluate new symptoms, try new treatments, and answer any questions that arise. The neurologist must often make referrals to other specialists, such as physical therapists and psychologists, so the patient should feel comfortable relying on these referrals and asking for additional ones as needed.

Health care plans that offer only a limited number of doctors to choose from can be problematic if the patient does not think a doctor approved by the plan is competent or caring. Sometimes financial concerns force a person to stick with what an insurance carrier dictates. If there is more flexibility, however, the patient and family must weigh the advantages and disadvantages of paying out of pocket for a doctor in whom they have more confidence.

Whichever physician a patient selects, MS advocates recommend making the most of each office visit by bringing a list of questions or concerns, keeping the doctor informed of new symptoms or adverse effects from medications, and inquiring about new research that may be helpful.

Strengthening Relationships

Along with establishing a good doctor-patient relationship, MS experts say that strengthening personal relationships can help patients on their journey with the disease. People who have stable,

An MS patient places a hand on his daughter's shoulder. Strong personal relationships can help those with multiple sclerosis cope with the hardships posed by the disease.

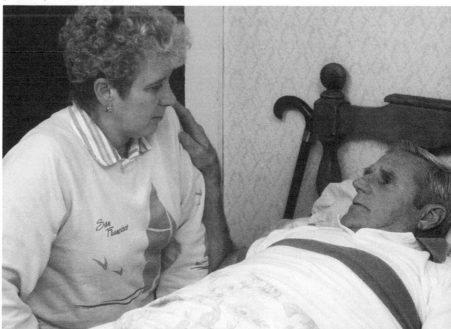

strong relationships with parents, a spouse, children, extended family, and friends tend to cope better with challenges that confront them; talking openly about MS and whatever stresses and feelings are associated with it is usually a good way of initiating a climate of cohesiveness.

Since everyone in a nuclear family is directly affected when one family member develops MS, another essential survival skill is for each individual to acknowledge and make necessary changes while not allowing the disease to totally disrupt all aspects of life. "The goal is to find a place for the illness while keeping the illness in its place,"[27] says Peter Steinglass, a psychiatrist who is an acclaimed expert on family issues arising from chronic illness.

Specific methods of achieving this goal include encouraging those in the family who wish to participate in activities no longer accessible to the person with MS to do so without feeling guilty, and recognizing the needs of each family member to have a life outside of caring for the MS patient. Sharing chores and hiring paid help if possible are good ways of preventing individuals from feeling overwhelmed by the need to assist the patient with daily activities.

Special Concerns for Children and Teens

Children and teens with a parent who has MS seem to be affected especially profoundly by the emotional and practical aspects of the disorder. Younger children often do not understand the nature of a disease like MS and may be frightened, angry, or confused by the affected parent's behavior or hospitalizations. Some children become obsessed with health and mortality issues.

Sometimes parents attempt to hide the truth about their MS from their kids; experts point out that the children sense something is wrong anyway and may often imagine that the parent is about to die. Explaining at an age-appropriate level that Mommy's legs feel like they have bricks inside or allowing the child to try out his father's wheelchair are methods of easing children's fears and establishing open lines of communication in a family. Providing children with age-appropriate books and videos about MS are also productive ways of helping.

An MS patient is surrounded by his family. Having a parent with MS poses special challenges for children and teens.

Teens who have a parent with MS also tend to experience emotional upheavals and may resent having to do extra chores around the house. Some teens whose ill parent depends on them for help with taking medicines and similar tasks worry about what will happen when they leave for college or get a job. Others feel embarrassed about having a parent who cannot walk or frustrated that the parent cannot do everything other parents can do. "Sometimes I can't figure out how I feel.... I get mad because Mom can't drive me places the way my friends' mothers do.... Then I feel bad for being angry because it's not her fault,"[28] says Mary, a young teen whose mother has MS.

Most teens find that talking about their concerns with their parents and seeking professional counseling and support group services if necessary can relieve some of the stress of living with MS. Being up front with friends also helps avoid embarrassment and awkwardness. Vicky, for instance, told some friends who were coming to her home that her mother was in a wheelchair. When they arrived, Vicky was grateful that her mom gave the friends a brief and humorous explanation of how her legs did not work well due to MS. Vicky's friends felt comfortable from that time forward and were happy to assist her mom in any way they could whenever they came to visit.

In general, scientific studies show that, despite the added stresses of having a parent with MS, most teens in such a situation end up emotionally stronger, more independent, more sensitive to the needs of others, and more aware of how fragile life is than are other teens.

Other Family Issues

Families also face many everyday issues beyond emotional coping and caring for a person with MS. Financial difficulties can bring stress and anxiety into a home because of the expense of diagnosing and treating MS, along with a possible loss of income from a disabled patient being unable to work. According to a study by the National Multiple Sclerosis Society, families report that worrying about medical insurance coverage caused almost as much stress in their daily lives as coping with the disease itself. Filing insurance claims, applying for government disability benefits, and paying for things like wheelchairs, at-home assistance for the MS patient, mental health care, and treatments not covered by insurance are among the financial issues that confront families.

While many people with MS can continue to work with possible interruptions during acute attacks, some must stop working altogether, particularly if they have the progressive form of the disease or if their job requires physical labor. Experts today encourage people to work as long as they are able, however, because studies show that continuing to work is emotionally good for patients who can do so.

Even those who continue to work, though, sometimes face on-the-job harassment or are denied promotions because of their illness. The Americans with Disabilities Act prohibits discrimination in hiring or promotions based on a disability like MS, but it is difficult, expensive, and time-consuming to prove that MS was the direct cause of someone's being denied a job or a promotion, or being fired.

Yet many MS patients have employers who go out of their way to offer support and accomodations for any special needs. Such situations, say affected people, make living with MS less stressful by removing one source of anxiety.

Living with Physical Limitations

Besides the potential loss of employment due to physical limitations, there are also many lifestyle adjustments people with MS confront because of these aspects of the disease. Many people tend to withdraw from normal activities after diagnosis, but experts say it is much better to stay as active as possible for as long as possible, within limits imposed by fatigue and other physical symptoms.

Physicians used to prescribe a lot of extra rest and no exercise for people with MS, but studies over the past few decades have shown that this is not necessary or desirable. One of the first public figures to challenge the recommendation of bed rest was Olympic skier Jimmie Heuga back in 1975. When Heuga was diagnosed with MS in 1970, his doctors told him to stop exercising. Heuga was so miserable that he devised his own workout schedule that included skiing. To his doctors' surprise, Heuga's strength, mobility, and outlook improved dramatically. Heuga began recruiting medical professionals to open a nonprofit organization that he named the Heuga Center. His goal was to fund MS research and to help other people with the disease live life to the fullest. Today, the Heuga Center has several facilities throughout the United States. Each year, specialists there custom-design activity, nutrition, and treatment plans for each patient who enrolls in the trademark CANDO program.

Based on Jimmie Heuga's pioneering work, many scientific studies have since confirmed the therapeutic value of different types of exercise. Today, experts recommend that people with MS choose a form of exercise they find enjoyable so they will do it on a regular basis to keep up their strength and sense of well-being. Of course, any exercise program must be flexible enough to accommodate the physical limitation imposed by MS and must ensure that the patient not get too overheated since this can worsen any disease symptoms.

Other Physical Adjustments

The adjustments MS patients must make because of physical limitations imposed by the disorder go well beyond incorporating

Jimmie Heuga, a 1964 Olympic bronze medalist in skiing who was diagnosed with MS in 1970, carries the Olympic torch prior to the 2002 Winter Games.

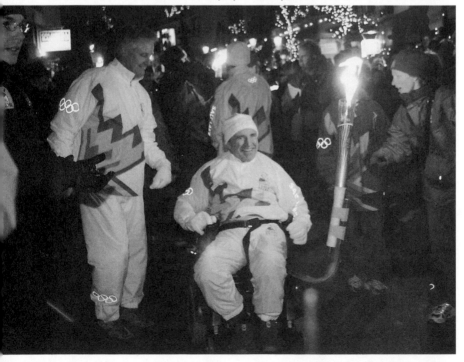

an appropriate daily exercise program. For example, problems with balance are frequent, and common sense suggests that those who fall easily should avoid walking on snow, ice, or slippery floors. In addition, families and other caregivers are advised to be sure that no objects are left lying around to trip over. Sturdy handrails on stairways and in bathrooms are a must.

Because of vision problems, dizziness, and weakness in the arms and legs, many people with MS are not able to drive a car, particularly during an acute attack. There may be resentment at having to rely on others for transportation, but often patients can resume driving once any dizziness, weakness, and vision loss subside. Many rehabilitation facilities have official testing centers where people can find out if and when they are ready to drive again. When permanent weakness in the legs makes driving difficult, a vehicle can be adapted to permit control entirely with the hands.

Another adjustment many people must make relates to the heat sensitivity that goes along with MS. Hot weather tends to bring on dizziness, weakness, or nausea, so most MS patients must be able to stay in a cool place at all times. Sunbathing, saunas, and hot tubs are out of the question. Fevers, another source of heat, can also trigger an acute attack, and this means that any cold or flulike illness must be carefully monitored to control the fever.

Social Adjustments and Long-Term Plans

The physical limitations brought about by MS have a tremendous influence on an individual's social functioning and long-term plans. Impaired balance, for example, can be socially embarrassing because it may be associated with intoxication. It may also be dangerous in crowded situations, so many people with MS avoid crowds. Busy places and noise tend to confuse patients with cognitive difficulties, so many restrict themselves to shopping when stores are not busy and to socializing with small groups of people.

Long-term planning presents even more of a dilemma than everyday social functioning. Most people learn to take things day by day and to see what they feel up to doing. Concerns such as planning a family, however, must be dealt with in advance and can present significant uncertainties for those involved. Although some research shows that pregnancy does not increase—and, in some cases, seems to decrease—the number of MS attacks, other data indicate that symptoms tend to worsen in the six months following childbirth, probably due to hormonal influences. Most doctors advise female patients that pregnancy usually does not affect the overall progression of the disease and is therefore safe to attempt. However, some of the medications used to treat MS can cause birth defects and must be discontinued before a woman becomes pregnant, introducing issues of timing and risk.

Many couples end up deciding against having children because of fears that the parent with MS may not be physically able to care for a child a few years down the road. Another consideration is the knowledge that susceptibility to multiple sclerosis has a genetic basis. A child who has a biological parent with MS is thirty times more likely to acquire the disorder than are other people.

Living with MS

With all of the practical, social, physical, and emotional aspects of life that MS disrupts, each day can offer challenges that healthy people rarely have to confront. However, many people with the disease manage to lead fulfilling lives thanks to improved medical treatments, emotional and practical support from health care professionals and support groups, and loving families who are there to help meet each crisis and deal with each day.

Chapter 5

The Future

A lthough medical science has made dramatic recent advances in improving the quality of life for people with multiple sclerosis, the disease continues to severely disable many individuals and causes incalculable suffering for patients and their families. However, a tremendous amount of ongoing research continues to increase knowledge about the disorder and offers hope that the future will bring innovations that make living with MS a less traumatic and unpredictable ordeal.

The National Multiple Sclerosis Society states that the goals of current research are to "speed the development of treatment, prevention and cure, understand disease process, prevent and reverse damage to the nervous system and improve function, and improve quality of life, care and delivery of medical services."[29]

Research into Causes

A great deal of research is currently devoted to explaining the causes of MS as a basis for understanding the disease process and for developing new methods of prevention and treatment. Scientists who are investigating this aspect of MS are focusing on how genetics, the immune system, and various environmental factors interact to produce the disease.

Genetic research is looking primarily at identifying the genes that make people susceptible to MS. As many as twenty genes may be involved in triggering the abnormalities that precede the autoimmune destruction of myelin. Several genetic screening studies are currently checking for differences between people who have MS and those who do not by examining the complete set of forty-six human chromosomes from thousands of volunteer subjects.

So far, it appears that at least two types of genes may be abnormal in people with MS: genes that help the immune system identify its own tissue as different from foreign substances and genes that control the T cell receptors that determine which substances these immune cells attack.

Scientists at a number of research centers are zeroing in on precisely which of the immune-regulating genes seem to be responsible for inducing MS. A project at the Georgetown University Medical Center in Washington, D.C., for example, is studying a gene known as Sp3 to find out why it appears to be inactive in people with MS. If it is proved that Sp3 regulates the immune system malfunctions that underlie the disease, a logical next step would be the development of methods of preventing and treating MS by activating this gene.

Genes and Environment

Other gene-oriented studies are attempting to find out why people who live in northern areas of the world seem to be more susceptible to developing MS. Scientists are not sure if this high susceptibility is due to genetics or environment, so they are looking at the genes of people who live or used to live in these northern regions with the goal of pinpointing any genetic patterns that might be used to predict who will get MS.

Other researchers are studying environmental factors that might protect people who live in certain areas. For example, a team of investigators at the University of Madison in Wisconsin is trying to determine why MS rarely occurs in areas near the equator, where poor sanitary conditions often prevail, exposing residents to constant low levels of parasitic infection. These researchers believe the explanation may be related to infections by certain microorganisms (parasites) that activate type 2 helper T cells (Th2 cells). The activity of Th2 cells might give protection against immune system chemicals that trigger the autoimmune destruction of myelin. Zsuasanna Fabry, a lead investigator on the team, explains: "Parasitic infections are very mild and common in areas of poor sanitary conditions. MS rarely occurs in these areas. We hypothesize that lack of exposure to such Th2-

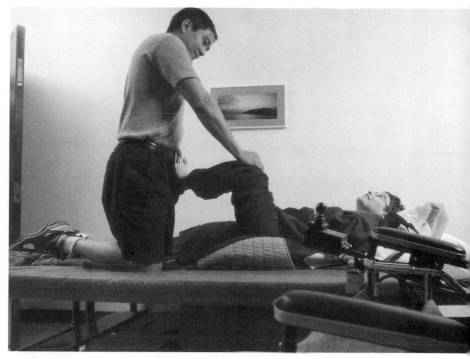

An MS patient receives physical therapy. Scientists continue to research the factors that contribute to the development of MS.

inducing infections in childhood is a critical environmental factor for the development of MS."[30]

Other research on environmental causes focuses on various viruses that have been tentatively linked to MS by antibodies in patients with the disease. So far, no virus has been proven to be responsible for causing the disorder, but scientists are still searching for likely candidates for their investigations.

The Autoimmune Process

Paralleling the projects investigating the genetic and environmental influences on MS, many current research efforts seek to determine exactly what malfunctions in the immune system are related to these influences. The ultimate goal of such research is to develop ways of suppressing only those parts of the immune system that trigger the autoimmune destruction of myelin. There are many ways of shutting off the entire immune system, but such methods leave the person open to infections and cancers. Thus, the idea is to target only certain mechanisms while leaving most of the immune functions intact.

One line of research in this direction focuses on how and why immune cells breach the blood-brain barrier. In a project at Yale University in New Haven, Connecticut, scientists are studying how T cells squeeze through blood vessels and migrate to the brain. The investigators believe that some migrating T cells congregate on blood vessel walls and stick there. Under certain conditions, enzymes called proteinases become active, breaking down the walls and allowing T cells to enter the nervous system. The researchers are attempting to find out what conditions activate this process and hope the research will lead to new methods of preventing and controlling MS.

Other studies relating to the autoimmune process are using magnetic resonance spectroscopy to analyze chemicals in body tissues. This powerful imaging technique has led to some clues about why some patients' immune systems continuously attack their myelin. Specifically, myelin that has not yet been attacked and appears normal under a conventional microscope may actually contain subtle abnormalities that can be detected with the more sophisticated magnetic resonance techniques. Researchers are proposing that perhaps these subtle myelin abnormalities are responsible for the continuous assault that leads to the progressive forms of MS. Further studies are underway to determine if this is indeed true.

Research on Individual Symptoms and Progression

Since scientists generally believe that the autoimmune attacks on myelin underlie the various forms of multiple sclerosis, many researchers are attempting to learn how attacks on this one substance, myelin, produce varying symptoms in different patients. A team of scientists led by Dr. Sara R. Abromson at the Harvard Medical School in Boston, Massachusetts, for example, has discovered that certain kinds of T cells in mice attack myelin in the

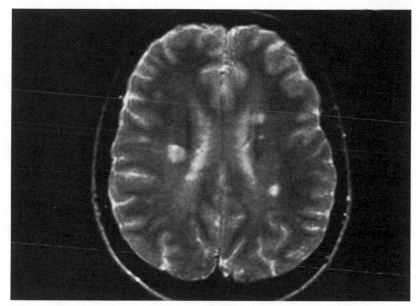

Some researchers theorize that chemicals in certain parts of the brain, shown here in a CAT scan, attract specific types of T cells, which destroy the myelin in those areas.

lower part of the brain, resulting in symptoms associated with that area. Other T cells target myelin in other brain regions, thereby triggering a variety of related symptoms. Abromson and her colleagues are trying to learn whether there are chemicals in certain parts of the brain that attract specific types of T cells.

Related research, known as the MS Lesion Project, is being conducted at the Mayo Clinic in Rochester, Minnesota, and at other research centers in an attempt to further probe the many forms of MS: Why do different people experience such different symptoms? The investigators study samples of MS lesions, or plaques, obtained by extracting a small amount of nerve tissue from patients' brains. The material harvested in this process, which is called a brain biopsy, is then analyzed in a laboratory.

Preliminary findings from these tests show that MS lesions from different people exhibit different patterns of myelin loss and varying levels of activity in proteins and immune cells. "Our findings suggest that there may be several types of MS, and that these types may have different immune-related causes. MS may prove to be a 'syndrome' of several diseases,"[31] explains lead researcher Dr. Claudia Luochinetti.

A team of investigators led by Dr. Guiseppe Santuccio in Milan, Italy, is also studying MS lesions and has discovered that patients with primary-progressive MS have fewer lesions but more axon damage than do patients with the secondary-progressive form of the disease. In addition, they have found that people with more damage in the neck area of the spinal cord experience more serious disability than do those with damage in other areas. Such findings could lead to improved diagnosis and treatments for certain varieties of the disorder.

Other new research on nerve damage focuses on the effects of the destruction of entire axons on MS symptoms and the long-term progression of the disease. For example, it is now thought that much of the irreversible disability that characterizes MS may be the result of axon damage; this is because axons normally do not repair themselves, but myelin sometimes does. Thus, dam-

Researchers think that damage to neurons such as these causes the permanent disability associated with MS.

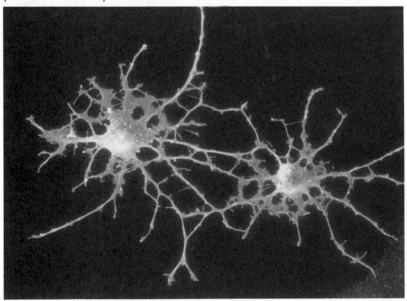

aged axons would almost inevitably result in permanent damage, whereas the chances of self-repair by myelin are somewhat better.

Research into New Treatments

As doctors learn more about the many chemicals, immune cells, and other factors important in the development of multiple sclerosis, this knowledge opens the door to new possibilities for treatment as well as prevention. One of the primary areas of investigation into new treatments involves creating and testing new drugs.

Initially, researchers develop new drugs in a laboratory and test these substances for safety and effectiveness on laboratory animals. Once a drug passes these tests, doctors begin clinical trials on humans. Most clinical trials are sponsored by a research institution like the National Institutes of Health or by a pharmaceutical company. They are set up at numerous hospitals and clinics throughout the world. Patients can find out about new trials through multiple sclerosis societies, journals, or from their physicians and may apply to participate if they wish.

Rules and regulations governing clinical trials are developed by the Food and Drug Administration (FDA) in the United States and by comparable organizations in other countries. Patients who participate do so voluntarily, with the understanding that the new treatment may or may not work for them. Before a drug can be approved for marketing, three or four trial phases must be completed in a satisfactory manner.

In the preliminary, or phase 1, studies, a small group of patients, usually no more than ten or twenty, receives the new drug to determine safe, effective doses; each person is also monitored for any adverse effects. Phase 2, also known as the pilot phase, recruits a larger group of patients, perhaps as many as one hundred, and administers the drug over several years. If the treatment does not appear to be beneficial, the clinical trial may be halted and the drug rejected or sent back to the laboratory for improvement. On the other hand, if the drug gives dramatic results and has few or no adverse effects in the short term, the FDA may assign it a so-called fast-track status that waives some of the lengthy testing requirements. This way, more people have access to promising treatments sooner.

In phase 3, thousands of patients are enrolled in the trial and are randomly assigned to either an experimental or a control group. People in the experimental group receive the new drug, but those in the control group are given a placebo, an inactive substance that looks like the real thing. Results from the control group indicate to statisticians whether any positive effects are due to the expectation of success rather than to the medication itself.

Patients, of course, are not informed about whether they are in the experimental or control group. This type of scientific study is known as a single-blind study. In some clinical trials, researchers go to even greater lengths to ensure unbiased results by doing a double-blind study, in which both doctors and patients are kept in the dark about who is in which group.

Upon successful completion of phase 3, the FDA may approve the new treatment for marketing. Further studies, called phase 4, or postmarket, studies may be arranged as well. Phase 4 studies are designed to learn more about adverse reactions to the drug, to test it on a related illness, or to recheck any questionable data from earlier studies.

Special Concerns with MS Clinical Trials

Because MS is such an unpredictable disease and because each patient shows wide variations in symptoms and progression, clinical trials tend to be more difficult to set up and interpret than are trials for many other diseases. The natural remissions typical of MS may be wrongly attributed to the new treatment. By the same token, recurrence can be misinterpreted as evidence that the treatment is worthless. A great deal of testing must be done on many patients before a drug can be considered truly effective or ineffective.

Since drugs are sometimes designed only to treat certain types of MS, selecting appropriate patients for clinical trials can also be challenging. For example, a drug being tested for use on progressive MS cannot be tested on people with the relapsing-remitting form of the disease. Yet often a relapsing-remitting disease will morph into secondary-progressive MS, changing a patient's disease status and perhaps making him or her eligible for the clinical trial.

Drugs Being Tested

A variety of medications to treat MS are currently in various stages of clinical trials. The anticancer drugs cladribine, methotrexate, and rituximab, for instance, seem to slow the progression of MS but have many dangerous effects; thus, they are being tested only on patients who have not been helped by other medications. Thalidomide, an immune system modulator famous for inducing birth defects when taken by pregnant women for morning sickness, appears to slow the course of MS and is being tested on patients with the primary-progressive form of the disease. The antibiotic minocycline, currently used to treat many infections, seems to reduce myelin inflammation in animals with experimental allergic encephalomyelitis (EAE) and is scheduled for phase 1 trials on people with MS at the University of Calgary in Canada. The influential British medical journal the *Lancet* reported on the projected study in 2002: "The investigators are

New medication may offer hope in successfully combating the debilitating symptoms of MS.

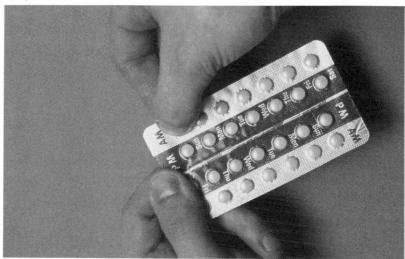

The venom from the Carribbean sea anemone has been shown to reverse paralysis in rats and may also help fight MS in humans.

optimistic about the potential of minocycline as a treatment for MS and its possible use in other demyelinating disorders."[32]

Also set to be tested on humans is venom from the Caribbean sea anemone, recently found by investigators at the University of California at Irvine to halt or reverse paralysis in rats with EAE. The venom appears to work by preventing T cells from attacking nerve cells, and scientists are hoping it will prove useful in treating MS as well.

Other substances being evaluated for their effectiveness in blocking the autoimmune process are man-made copies of naturally occurring body chemicals. One naturally occurring cytokine that may help arrest the progression of MS is interleukin-10; another is a protein of the immune system known as gamma globulin. Testing on these substances is only beginning, and results are inconclusive.

Besides drugs to slow the progression of MS, several drugs are being studied to treat specific symptoms. Examples are Prokarin, administered by a skin patch, which shows promise for alleviating fatigue; and Cylert, presently used to treat fatigue, which may be helpful in reducing some of the cognitive problems experienced by many MS patients.

New Combinations and Methods of Administration for Existing Drugs

In addition to testing new drugs for MS, doctors are also experimenting with new drug combinations and ways of administering existing medications. For example, combinations of Avonex and Copaxone and of Betaseron and Novantrone, all currently used individually to slow the progression of MS, are being tried for the purpose of learning whether combining these medications is more effective than using each drug alone.

Several groups of researchers are testing forms of interferon beta that can be administered by mouth or by nose. Such delivery options would free patients from present regimens of frequent injections.

Another experimental use of existing MS drugs involves testing whether interferon beta and interferon beta 1-a might be effective in treating the progressive forms of the disease in addition to the relapsing-remitting form. Preliminary results with Avonex indicate that using twice the usual dosage may be therapeutic for secondary-progressive MS; and additional testing is planned to determine if this regimen will be useful for primary-progressive MS as well.

New Forms of Treatment Using Myelin

Evaluating a variety of new and existing drugs is just one avenue of current research that promises to improve treatment of multiple sclerosis in the near future; some scientists are studying entirely new methods of arresting the disease.

One experimental technique known as inducing immunologic tolerance involves giving MS patients myelin proteins by mouth. The rationale behind this is that substances ingested orally are not usually recognized by the immune system as foreign antigens. Food, for example, is technically foreign matter to an eater's body, but food is not normally attacked by immune cells. Researchers reason that if myelin proteins are taken by mouth, like food, perhaps the MS patient's body will stop destroying them, thereby preventing attacks.

Other experimental treatments using myelin involve testing ways of helping this protective sheath repair itself after it has been damaged. One line of investigation is looking at how and why oligodendrocytes, the cells that make myelin, seem to switch off and not regenerate after acute MS attacks. Scientists at several research centers, including the University of Cincinnati in Ohio and the Memorial Sloan-Kettering Cancer Institute in New York, are studying how immature oligodendrocytes, known as progenitor cells, might be stimulated to begin myelin repair. Other researchers are exploring the use of chemical growth factors, called neuregulins, to signal the appropriate cells to start producing new myelin.

Another important avenue of investigation is trying to develop ways of transplanting healthy myelin into people with MS. In 2001 researchers at Yale University performed the first such procedure by transplanting myelin-producing cells from areas of the nervous system outside the brain and spinal cord into plaques in the brains of several MS patients. The results of this study have not yet been released, but the doctors have high

A microscopic image shows the destruction of myelin sheaths. One experimental technique doctors are researching is the ingestion of myelin protein by mouth.

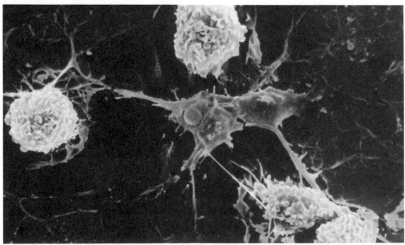

hopes that, if the technique works, it will represent a huge step forward. The challenge in perfecting an effective transplant procedure, according to researcher Jeffrey Kocsis, is finding the right cells for the job:

> This is a major effort right now, with researchers investigating a variety of cell types. First, we need to show that the cell can survive—transplanting any organ or cell carries the risk of rejection, in which the immune system attacks the new tissue. We also need to make sure that the cell will develop without abnormalities. Finally, we need to determine if the cell can migrate to areas of myelin damage and form new tissue.[33]

Other Experimental Methods

Two other cutting-edge experimental techniques are plasma exchange and bone marrow transplantation. In plasma exchange, doctors remove as much of the patient's plasma—the liquid portion of blood—as possible and replace it with artificial plasma made of a salt and protein solution. This is achieved using a plasmapheresis machine, which withdraws one-half to one-and-a-half cups of blood at a time from one vein, separates the plasma from the blood cells, discards the plasma, mixes the remaining blood cells with the artificial plasma, and returns the new mixture to the patient's body through a second intravenous tube. The process is repeated for several hours, and often multiple sessions are required to free the person's blood of its natural plasma.

The rationale behind the technique is that since natural plasma contains antibodies and other immune chemicals that attack myelin, replacing it with artificial plasma should inhibit the autoimmune process.

Preliminary results in a study at the Mayo Clinic found that MS patients who received seven plasma exchanges over two weeks showed improvements in MS-related disabilities, though the individuals did become anemic from a loss of red blood cells. Doctors hope the procedure can be refined to avoid this problem and will prove beneficial for people who do not respond to standard therapies.

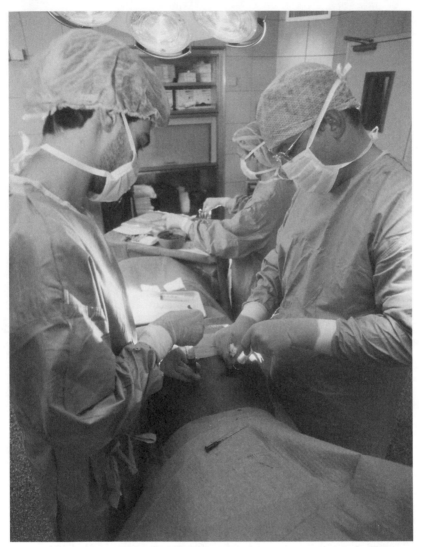

Surgeons harvest bone marrow for a transplant.

Bone marrow transplantation, currently used to treat some forms of cancer, is another procedure now being tested on people with MS who are not helped by other treatments. Bone marrow, which is the soft, spongy tissue inside bones that manufactures blood cells, is destroyed and replaced with new marrow grown from the patient's own cells or from another person's marrow.

The transplanted marrow has none of the immune cells that attack myelin; thus, it can potentially arrest the progression of MS. Such transplants are extremely risky, and many patients die from complications, but they may offer a chance of improvement for patients in desperate condition.

Research into Quality-of-Life Issues

In addition to the many research projects attempting to develop improved treatment techniques, experts are also studying methods of bettering access to medical care and quality of life in general for MS patients. One area of concern is that recent research indicates that numerous patients who require extensive full-time care are abused or neglected by family members or paid caregivers. This finding has led advocacy groups to initiate efforts to educate caregivers about the needs and rights of patients and to alert social services and law enforcement organizations about the widespread existence of varying levels of emotional and physical abuse and neglect.

MS experts realize that there is room for improvement in quality of care for patients in general, even in the many cases in which no abuse or neglect exists. A large-scale study that is under way to address this issue is the Sonya Slifka Longitudinal Multiple Sclerosis Study, funded by the National Multiple Sclerosis Society. This research is named in honor of a prominent contributor to the society and represents the first-ever large-scale attempt to follow a sample of over two thousand patients across the United States. The investigators are studying many factors related to access to treatment, the disease process, social and family issues, geographic data, financial considerations, and other quality-of-life concerns. Their goal is to follow the patients for several years and to make recommendations for improving these aspects of MS care.

Is There a Cure in Sight?

As researchers and health care professionals continue to make advancements in understanding and treating multiple sclerosis, the question of when and how the disease can eventually be cured comes up more frequently. Experts agree that at this point it is impossible to predict how long it might be before a cure is discovered. The National Multiple Sclerosis Society outlines the magnitude of the task: "In order to develop a tree cure for MS, that is, a treatment that will reverse symptoms and restore the patient's former level of function, a multi-step process would be

While a cure may be years away, treatments for MS allow those who must live with the disease to enjoy a better life.

involved, including halting demyelination, prompting remyelination, and repairing damaged axons."[34]

Although it is not possible to say when and if such a cure will materialize, people who live and work with multiple sclerosis have good reason to be optimistic in this era of unprecedented breakthroughs in research and treatment. The authors of *Multiple Sclerosis: A Guide for the Newly Diagnosed* sum up the issue: "What we can say in general terms is that the outlook is improving year by year and will continue to improve. Research is proceeding rapidly, and although it will never be fast enough or great enough for those suffering daily with multiple sclerosis, we are heading in the right direction."[35]

Notes

Introduction: An Unpredictable and Incurable Disease

1. Nancy Holland, T. Jock Murray, and Stephen C. Reingold, *Multiple Sclerosis: A Guide for the Newly Diagnosed*. New York: Demos Vermande, 1996, p. 4.

2. Quoted in Holland, Murray, and Reingold, *Multiple Sclerosis*, p. 54.

3. Roger S. Cicala, *The Brain Disorders Sourcebook*. Los Angeles: Lowell House, 1999, p. vii.

4. Quoted in National Multiple Sclerosis Society, "Highlight: Spotlight on the Hartzler Family," *Inside MS*. www.nation almssociety.org.

5. Quoted in Holland, Murray, and Reingold, *Multiple Sclerosis*, p. xi.

Chapter 1: What Is Multiple Sclerosis?

6. Quoted in P.J. Vinken and B.W. Bruyn, eds., *Multiple Sclerosis and Other Demyelinating Diseases*. Amsterdam: North Holland, 1970, p. 46.

7. Cicala, *The Brain Disorders Sourcebook*, p. 333.

8. Doug Carroll, interview by author, Cayucos, California, March 27, 2002.

9. Quoted in David L. Carroll and Jon Dudley Dorman, *Living Well with MS*. New York: HarperPerennial, 1993, p. 31.

10. Cicala, *The Brain Disorders Sourcebook*, p. 339.

Chapter 2: What Causes Multiple Sclerosis?

11. National Multiple Sclerosis Society, "Sourcebook—Etiology." www.nationalmssociety.org.

12. Holland, Murray, and Reingold, *Multiple Sclerosis,* p. 14.

13. Quoted in *Pain and Central Nervous System Week,* "Epstein-Barr Virus Associated with Increased Risk of Multiple Sclerosis," January 7, 2002, p. 9.

14. Quoted in *Pain and Central Nervous System Week,* "Epstein-Barr Virus," p. 9.

Chapter 3: How Is Multiple Sclerosis Treated?

15. National Multiple Sclerosis Society, "Sourcebook—Early Intervention." www.nationalmssociety.org.

16. National Multiple Sclerosis Society, "Sourcebook—Early Intervention."

17. Randall Schapiro, "Treatment Overview." www.ms-doctors.org.

18. Cicala, *The Brain Disorders Sourcebook,* p. 357.

Chapter 4: Living with Multiple Sclerosis

19. Chris Lombardi, "Faces: Jimmie Heuga—Changing the Face of MS," *Inside MS,* Fall 2001. www.nationalmssociety.org.

20. Holland, Murray, and Reingold, *Multiple Sclerosis,* p. 52.

21. Quoted in Holland, Murray, and Reingold, *Multiple Sclerosis,* p. 51.

22. Carroll and Dorman, *Living Well with MS,* p. 68.

23. Quoted in Carroll and Dorman, *Living Well with MS,* p. 225.

24. Quoted in Holland, Murray, and Reingold, *Multiple Sclerosis,* p. 62.

25. Carroll, interview.

26. Carroll and Dorman, *Living Well with MS,* p. 200.

27. Quoted in Rosalind C. Kalb, *Multiple Sclerosis: A Guide for Families.* New York: Demos Vermande, 1998, p. 7.

28. Quoted in Pamela Cavallo with Martha Jablow, "When a Parent Has MS: A Teenager's Guide." www.nationalmssociety.org.

Chapter 5: The Future

29. National Multiple Sclerosis Society, "About Research—Fact Sheet." www.nationalmssociety.org.

30. Quoted in National Multiple Sclerosis Society, "Research Highlights, Fall 2001." www.nationalmssociety.org.

31. Quoted in Sara Silberman, "The MS Lesion Project: Taking the Mystery Out of MS," *Inside MS,* Winter 2001. www.nation almssociety.org.

32. Rebecca Love, "Potential Antibiotic Treatment for Multiple Sclerosis," *Lancet,* January 5, 2002, p. 50.

33. Quoted in National Multiple Sclerosis Society, "Research Highlights, Summer 2001." www.nationalmssociety.org.

34. National Multiple Sclerosis Society, "Sourcebook—Outlook for a Cure." www.nationalmssociety.org.

35. Holland, Murray, and Reingold, *Multiple Sclerosis,* p. 10.

Glossary

antibody: A chemical produced by the immune system to neutralize an antigen.

antigen: A foreign substance that triggers an immune response.

autoimmune response: Attacks on the body's own cells by its immune system.

axon: The main branching filament and conductor of electrical impulses on a nerve cell.

blood-brain barrier: A biological mechanism that prevents substances in the blood from entering the central nervous system.

cerebrospinal fluid: The liquid that protects the brain and spinal cord.

clinical trial: A scientific study to test new treatments on patients.

cytokine: Chemicals that regulate the activities of immune cells.

demyelination: Destruction of the myelin tissue that protects nerve cells.

dendrite: The thin branches of a nerve cell.

evoked potential: Measurement of the electrical activity of nerves.

gene: The basic unit of hereditary information.

incontinence: The inability to control urination.

intravenous: Injected or dripped into a vein.

lesion: The area of cell destruction.

myelin: A protective fatty sheath on nerve cell branches.

neurological: Affecting the nervous system.

neurologist: A physician who specializes in the diagnosis and treatment of diseases of the nervous system.

neuron: A nerve cell.

neurotransmitter: A chemical messenger released by a neuron.

oligodendrocytes: Cells that manufacture myelin.

plaque: The area of demyelination on a nerve cell.

sclerosis: Scarring; in MS, the result of plaque formation.

spasm: The sudden, uncontrollable contraction of muscles; frequent spasms lead to the condition known as spasticity.

Organizations to Contact

Heuga Center
27 Main St., Suite 303
Edwards, CO 81632
(800) 367-3101
www.heuga.org

The Heuga Center funds research and offers comprehensive medical programs for people with MS.

MS Awareness Foundation (MSAF)
PO Box 1193
Venice, FL 34284
(888) 336-6723
www.msawareness.org

The MSAF offers information and support on all aspects of living with MS for patients and families.

Multiple Sclerosis Association of America (MSAA)
706 Haddonfield Rd.
Cherry Hill, NJ 08002
(800) LEARN MS
www.msaa.com

The MSAA provides general information and direct services for patients and families; it also maintains a nationwide registry of support groups.

Multiple Sclerosis Foundation (MSF)
6350 N. Andrews Ave.
Fort Lauderdale, FL 33309-2130

(800) 225-6495

www.msfacts.org

The MSF offers comprehensive information on MS causes, diagnosis, treatment, research, and support services.

National Multiple Sclerosis Society (NMSS)

733 Third Ave.

New York, NY 10017

(800) 344-4867

info@nmss.org

www.nationalmssociety.org

The NMSS provides comprehensive information on the causes, diagnosis, and treatment of MS as well as research, news bulletins, an online library, and links to support groups and local chapters.

For Further Reading

Books

Chamein T. Canton, *MS. Doesn't Stand for Multiple Sclerosis.* Lincoln, NE: Universe, 2000. An upbeat first-person account of a woman's journey with multiple sclerosis.

Barbara Cristall, *Coping When a Parent Has Multiple Sclerosis.* New York: Rosen, 1992. A family guide for dealing with a parent who has MS.

Susan Dudley Gold, *Multiple Sclerosis.* Berkeley Heights, NJ: Enslow, 2001. Written for teens; discusses causes, diagnosis, treatment, and the human side of MS.

Paul O'Connor, *Multiple Sclerosis: The Facts You Need.* Willowdale, Ontario, Canada: Firefly Books, 1999. A comprehensive guide for people who live with multiple sclerosis.

Websites

International Multiple Sclerosis Support Foundation
(www.aspin.asu.edu/msnews/mssf.htm.) An online support group run by volunteers.

Med Support FSF International
(www.medsupport.org). An online newsgroup and monthly newsletter for patients and families.

Works Consulted

Books

David L. Carroll and Jon Dudley Dorman, *Living Well with MS.* New York: HarperPerennial, 1993. An easily understood guide to living with MS.

Roger S. Cicala, *The Brain Disorders Sourcebook.* Los Angeles: Lowell House, 1999. This book covers brain anatomy, function, and diseases; it also has extensive information on MS.

Nancy Holland, T. Jock Murray, and Stephen C. Reingold, *Multiple Sclerosis: A Guide for the Newly Diagnosed.* New York: Demos Vermande, 1996. This work covers all aspects of MS, especially lifestyle and coping issues.

Rosalind C. Kalb, *Multiple Sclerosis: A Guide for Families.* New York: Demos Vermande, 1998. A very detailed guide for families affected by MS, including legal, medical, and lifestyle issues.

P.J. Vinken and G.W. Bruyn, eds., *Multiple Sclerosis and Other Demyelinating Diseases.* Amsterdam: North Holland, 1970. A highly technical medical school textbook; it offers a good section on the history of multiple sclerosis.

Periodicals

Maria Pia Amato, "Cognitive Dysfunction in Early-Onset Multiple Sclerosis: A Reappraisal After Ten Years," *Journal of the American Medical Association,* January 2, 2002.

Donald H. Gilden, "Viruses and Multiple Sclerosis," *Journal of the American Medical Association,* December 26, 2001.

Health and Medicine Week, "Intranasal Interferon (beta) Phase 1 Clinical Trial Initiated (by Nastech Pharmaceutical Company Inc)," December 31, 2001.

Immunotherapy Weekly, "Scientists Ponder Why Immune System Protein Accelerates MS (Multiple Sclerosis Progression Accelerated by Osteopontin)," December 19, 2001.

———, "Sea Anemone Toxin Halts Experimental Disease," December 12, 2001.

Rebecca Love, "Potential Antibiotic Treatment for Multiple Sclerosis," *Lancet*, January 5, 2002.

Pain and Central Nervous System Week, "Epstein-Barr Virus Associated with Increased Risk of Multiple Sclerosis." January 7, 2002.

Internet Sources

Pamela Cavallo with Martha Jablow, "When a Parent Has MS: A Teenager's Guide." www.nationalmssociety.org.

Chris Lombardi, "Faces: Jimmie Heuga—Changing the Face of MS," *Inside MS*, Fall 2001. www.nationalmssociety.org.

Multiple Sclerosis Association of America, "What Is MS?" www.msaa.com.

Multiple Sclerosis Foundation, "MS Info." www.msfacts.org.

National Multiple Sclerosis Society, "About Research—Fact Sheet." www.nationalmssociety.org.

———, "Bone Marrow Transplantation for Treatment of Severe Multiple Sclerosis."

———, "Epidemiology."

———, "Highlight: Spotlight on the Hartzler Family," *Inside MS*.

———, "New Report on Possible Association of Stress with Multiple Sclerosis."

———, "New Research."

———, "Progress in Research."

———, "Research Highlights, Fall 2001."

———, "Research Highlights, Summer 2001."

———, "Sourcebook—Early Intervention."

———, "Sourcebook—Etiology."

———, "Sourcebook—Outlook for a Cure."

————, "Study Suggests Plasma Exchange May Help Severe MS Attacks."

————, "Summary of Research Progress—2001."

————, "$10.7 Million Awarded for New MS Research Projects."

————, "Trauma."

————, "What Causes MS?"

Loren A. Rolak, "MS: An Historical Perspective." www.national mssociety.org.

Randall Schapiro, "Treatment Overview." www.ms-doctors.org.

Sara Silberman, "The MS Lesion Project: Taking the Mystery Out of MS," *Inside MS*, Winter 2001. www.nationalmssociety. org.

Index

Picture Credits

About the Author

Melissa Abramovitz grew up in San Diego, California, and developed an interest in medical topics as a teenager. She began college with the intention of becoming a doctor, but she later switched majors and graduated summa cum laude from the University of California, San Diego, with a degree in psychology in 1976.

She launched her career as a writer in 1986 to allow her to be an at-home mom when her two children were small, realized she had found her niche in life, and continues to write regularly for a variety of magazines and educational book publishers. In her sixteen years as a freelancer, she has published hundreds of nonfiction articles and numerous short stories, poems, and books for children, teenagers, and adults. Many of her works are on medical topics.

At the present time Abramovitz lives in San Luis Obispo, California, with her husband, two teenaged sons, and two extremely spoiled dogs.